THE LITTLE

Local Government Fraud Prevention

How to *Prevent* It
How to *Detect* It

CHARLES HALL
CPA, CFE, MAcc

THE LITTLE BOOK OF LOCAL GOVERNMENT FRAUD
PREVENTION

Book design and production by Michael C. Koiner,
Koiner Co. LLC.

ISBN-13: 978-1496048493
ISBN-10: 1496048490

CONTENTS

Preface

The *Little Book of Local Government Fraud Prevention* is written for both the professional fraud examiner and layman alike. Since most fraud books are too long and too technical, I've made this book short and practical—you should finish your read within two or three hours. Even if you know little about fraud, you will soon have a much better understanding of how it's carried out and why it happens. For the professional fraud examiner, you will find easy-to-understand prevention and detection techniques. And given the penchant that CPAs and fraud examiners have for checklists, I've also included those.

The journey we are to take includes:

- Local Government Fraud—An Overview
- General Local Government Fraud Prevention
- Cash Receipts and Billing Fraud
- Disbursement and Purchasing Fraud
- Payroll Fraud
- Capital Asset Fraud
- Detecting Fraud
- Procuring Fraud-Related Audit Services
- Auditing and Certified Public Accountants
- Supplemental Information (checklists and resources)

Who will find the book helpful?

- Local government accounting personnel
- Local government administrative personnel
- Elected officials
- Local government auditors
- Local government attorneys
- Certified Public Accountants
- Certified Fraud Examiners

Together—as elected officials, local government employees, and auditors—we can protect our cities, towns, counties, authorities, and other local governments from theft.

Come join the journey. We'll all be better for it.

Macon, Georgia
February 15, 2014

*To my wife, Kelley, the love of my life,
and my two dear children, Spencer and Madison.*

Introduction

$53 MILLION AND SOME CHANGE

Rita Crundwell, comptroller and treasurer of Dixon, Illinois, stole $53 million over a twenty-year period. The city of 16,000 residents held Crundwell in high esteem. One friend described her as "sweet as pie." Another said: "You could not find a nicer person."

So why did she steal?

It appears Rita simply enjoyed the good life. She used the money to fund one of the top quarter horse ranches in the country, and she did it with style: Some of the funds were used to purchase over $300,000 worth of jewelry and a $2.1 million motor coach vehicle.

Her annual salary? $80,000.

The city's annual budget? $6 to $8 million

Were annual audits performed? Yes.

Were annual audit reports submitted to state officials? Yes.

Were budgets approved? Yes.

So how could this happen? Ms. Crundwell had won the trust of those around her—especially that of the mayor and council. In April 2011, finance commissioner and veteran council member, Roy Bridgeman, praised Crundwell calling her "a big asset to the city as she looks after every tax dollar as if it were her own."

It was a disturbing moment when Dixon Mayor James Burke presented the FBI with evidence of Crundwell's fraud. Burke later recalled his emotions and words: "I literally became sick to my stomach, and I told him that I hoped my suspicions were all wrong." Such a response is understandable given that Crundwell had worked for the city for decades. She had fooled everyone.

According to the mayor, the city's annual audits raised no red flags, and the city's main bank never reported anything suspicious.

So how did she steal the money?

In 1990, Crundwell opened a secret bank account in the name of the city (titled the RSDCA account: the initials stood for *reserve sewer development construction account*). Crundwell was the only authorized check signer for the account, and the RSDCA bank account was never set up on the city's general ledger. No deposits to or disbursements from this account were recorded on the city's records.

Crundwell would write and sign manual checks from a legitimate city capital project fund checking account, completing the check payee line with "Treasurer." (Yes, Crundwell had the authority to issue checks with just her signature—even for legitimate city bank accounts.) She would then deposit the check into her secret account. From the bank's perspective, a transfer had been made from one city bank account to another (from the capital projects fund to the reserve sewer development construction fund).

While the capital project fund disbursement was recorded on the city's books, the RSDCA deposit was not. A capital project fund journal entry was made for each check, debiting capital outlay expense and crediting cash. But no entry was made to the city's records for the deposit to the RSDCA account. Once the money was in the RSDCA account, Crundwell wrote checks for personal expenses—and she did so for over twenty years.

To complete her deceit, Crundwell provided auditors with fictitious invoices from the Illinois Department of

Transportation. These invoices included the following notation: *Please make checks payable to Treasurer, State of Illinois.* (So the canceled checks made out to *Treasurer* agreed with the directions on the invoice, but the words *State of Illinois* were conveniently left off the check payee line.) Remember Crundwell was the treasurer of Dixon. Those invoices and the related checks were often for round dollar amounts (e.g., $250,000) and most were for more than $100,000. In one year alone, Crundwell embezzled over $5 million.

So how was she caught?

While Rita was on an extended vacation for horse shows, the city hired a replacement for her. For some reason, Crundwell's substitute requested *all* bank account statements from the city's bank. As those statements were reviewed, the secret bank account was discovered, and soon thereafter the mayor contacted the FBI.

Today Rita sits alone in a Minnesota prison; her sentence is 19.5 years. The auditors and the bank were sued by the city of Dixon and in September 2013, the parties reached a $40 million settlement with $10 million going to legal fees. Also the U.S. Marshals Service generated $10 million in proceeds from the sale of Crundwell's property. These actions enabled the city to recoup much of the stolen funds, but oh, the pain and embarrassment.

Why did the government officials not detect the fraud? How could a fraud exist for over 20 years without detection? Is fraud—like this one, but smaller in size—occurring in your own government?

To control the potential effects of fraud, it's important we understand where fraud occurs and how. While fraud manifests itself in many forms, when equipped with the right knowledge, you can protect your government from theft.

CHAPTER 1

Local Government Fraud – An Overview

Before we dig into fraud at the ground level of individual transactions, let's take a look at local government fraud from 30,000 feet. We need to understand the big picture before drilling deeper—at the transaction level—where fraud really happens. To initially develop our understanding of governmental fraud, let's examine:

- Who steals
- The language of fraud
- Where fraud occurs
- How and why fraud occurs

Thou Shalt Not Steal

I learned it in Sunday school: *Thou shalt not steal*. I knew better, but the temptation of taking one of my father's five-dollar bills was too great. Besides, he'd never know—he had so many five-dollar bills. My little mind rationalized, "He won't even miss it." And surely I, a five-year old, needed the money more than my father. So I took and hid, as so many throughout history have done (Al Capone, Bonnie and Clyde, and now, freckled-faced south Georgia boy Charles Hall).

My secret hiding place was a red stamp box in the hallway of our home. My father must have found it. On the way to our Florida vacation, he asked, "Who took five dollars from my billfold?" First silence filled the air...then my sister chimed in, "Not me," and in rapid staccato fashion, my two brothers yelled "Not me either." Hoping to hide my guilt, I quickly retorted "Not me" and glanced around the car as if to say, "Who *could* have done this?"

It was then I had the most vexing vacation of my life. I couldn't tell my father. Like Ralphie from *A Christmas Story*, I imagined my Dad would kill me. It was only upon arriving back home that I confessed, and my father swept me up in his arms saying, "Son, I knew it was you all along." (Thankfully, he did not kill me.) As a kid, I learned my lesson. Some adults never do. So what does a typical fraudster look like?

The Poster Child

Through the years, I've seen people from diverse social, ethnic, and age groups steal. Even so, fraud studies point to one consistent picture of the typical fraudster. And what is that picture? He looks like me. He's male, educated, in a position of authority, and has been on the payroll for a while.

The Association of Certified Fraud Examiners (ACFE), in its 2012 *Report to the Nations* (a fraud survey), indicates the following about those who steal:

- Roughly two-thirds of frauds are committed by males.
- The median fraud loss from males is $200,000; the median loss from females is $91,000.
- Approximately 54% of all fraudsters are between the ages of 31 and 45; fraud losses tend to rise with the age of the perpetrator.
- Approximately 42% of fraudsters have between one and five years of tenure at their organizations; fewer than 6% of perpetrators commit fraud within the first year on the job.
- 54% of fraudsters have a college degree or higher.

- Fraud schemes committed by those in executive/upper management cause the largest median losses.

My observation is that there is greater diversity in governments, so the above statistics may not be as relevant. Rather than trying to identify fraudsters by typical characteristics (e.g., gender or education), I like to consider:
- Who are the trusted employees with authority?
- What can they do?
- Who fully understands the accounting system?

A fraudster is frequently the person you would *not* expect to steal: the trusted employee, the individual who has been around the longest, the one who understands and controls accounting (remember Rita Crundwell). The trusted, long-time staff member is usually accorded greater control—*because* he or she is seen as trustworthy. This person has the keys to the kingdom.

Additionally, I've noticed that elected officials fit this "trusted" category, and some take advantage of the power they possess to circumvent internal controls. For example, who is going to question the sheriff? When one person—regardless of who he or she is—has full control of the accounting process, be careful!

So why is the trusted employee the one who commonly steals?

Because he can.

You may be thinking: *Duh?* But this is a critical point. As we will soon see, this dynamic—referred to as *opportunity*—is a key component of fraud.

While in France

Once while I was traveling in France, I was looking for a train station. I stopped a kind elderly gentleman on the street and asked, in English, for directions. I soon realized we were not understanding one another. In my frustration, I began to say, "toot, toot!" He smiled (thinking "crazy American") and pointed; soon I reached my destination. In this instance, I was able to overcome the language barrier. But to make our fraud journey easier, we need a common language. So please allow me to define the following terms:

- Fraud
- Abuse
- Asset misappropriation
- Corruption
- Financial statement fraud
- Fraud prevention
- Fraud detection

Fraud—What Is It?

I recently read of a southern city that had undocumented expenses of $200 million over a twelve-year period. Is this fraud? Not necessarily. In this instance, you need to demonstrate that funds were stolen before you can prove fraud. Though a red flag, the lack of invoice support does not prove that theft occurred.

In another example, Bobby Johnson, the CFO of a hospital authority, recently changed the method of calculating the allowance for uncollectible accounts. The change resulted in a positive change in net income of $1.2 million dollars. Is this fraudulent reporting? It all depends. Governments can and sometimes should change how they compute estimates. Did Bobby change the computation to juice up net income? Or does the change more accurately reflect the hospital authority's environment? It's not always easy to know. But remember this: to prove fraud, you must prove *intent*. If Bobby did not *intend* to misrepresent the numbers, fraud does not exist. An error in judgment? Possibly, but no fraud.

The Association of Certified Fraud Examiners defines occupational fraud as:

"The use of one's occupation for personal enrichment through the deliberate misuse or misapplication of the employing organization's resources or assets."

Personally I define fraud as:
- Money is stolen, or
- Financial statements are intentionally misstated (also known as "cooking the books")

Three Fraud Categories

The ACFE categorizes fraud as follows:

1. ***Asset misappropriation*** schemes: An employee steals or misuses the organization's resources (e.g., theft of company cash, false billing schemes, or inflated expense reports)
2. ***Corruption*** schemes: An employee misuses his or her influence in a business transaction in a way that violates his or her duty to the employer in order to gain a direct or indirect benefit (e.g., schemes involving bribery or conflicts of interest)
3. ***Financial statement fraud*** schemes: An employee intentionally causes a misstatement or omission of material information in the organization's financial reports (e.g., intentionally recording fictitious revenues or understating expenses)

Abuse—What Is It?

Another closely related term is *abuse*. Think of abuse as a lesser form of fraud, though the distinction between the two can sometimes blur.

Examples of abuse include:
- Employees calling in sick when they are well

- Employees driving public vehicles for personal purposes
- Employees making excessive personal phone calls during work hours
- Employees taking government-owned equipment home for personal use
- Employees using the government's copy machines for personal projects or businesses

This book mainly deals with fraud rather than abuse; nevertheless, consider that both occur, and that you may need to craft abuse-related preventive policies in addition to your fraud prevention measures.

Fraud Prevention and Detection

Fraud-related internal controls are commonly broken down into two categories:
- Fraud prevention
- Fraud detection

Prevention is usually the more costly of the two, but it is more effective. As the name states, these procedures are designed to stop fraud before it occurs. An example of a prevention procedure is the review of direct deposit bank account numbers for potential duplicates prior to payroll processing.

By contrast, detection measures are performed after transactions are processed (and after fraud may have taken place). As you might expect, these controls tend to be less expensive and less cumbersome to administer. An example of a detection procedure is the review of W-2s at year-end for excessive payments.

We've now defined our fraud terms, so let's examine the *nature* of fraud. What types of theft are most common? How long do most schemes last? What are the ingredients of fraud?

Which Fraud Is More Common?

Theft is the most common type of fraud in governments. Money can be stolen directly (e.g., skimming) or indirectly (e.g., bribery). Funds can be stolen by those *with* direct access to cash (e.g., a receipting clerk) and by those *without* direct access to cash (e.g., elected officials).

Financial statement fraud is not common in most local governments. Are there misstatements? Yes. Are the misstatements intentional? Usually no. The misstatements are normally mistakes rather than manipulation. Public sector entities simply have fewer incentives to manipulate the financial statements than their private-sector counterparts. For instance, a publicly-held company may manipulate profits in order to increase stock prices, but public entities don't have this temptation.

Incentives for manipulating governmental financial statements do increase as public entities grow in size. Complex investment and debt agreements can tempt governments to manipulate numbers, especially when financial conditions have deteriorated. Complexity (e.g., interest rate swaps) may provide enough opacity to hide the nonrecognition of adverse financial events. And governments with debt may have certain financial statement requirements known as debt covenants that increase the temptation to cheat on the numbers.

Though auditors should consider the possibility of financial statement fraud, this book focuses primarily on the more prevalent forms of governmental fraud: asset misappropriation and corruption.

Average Local Government Fraud Damages

The ACFE's biennial fraud survey usually reports median governmental per-case damages in the range of $80,000 to $100,000, but fraud committed by upper-level management can easily exceed $1 million depending on the size of the government. As we saw in the Rita Crundwell story, Dixon,

Illinois, a city of just 16,000, was defrauded of over $53 million.

Given that the *2012 Census of Governments* identifies approximately 89,000 U.S. local governments, there are a great number of counties, cities, towns, school districts, and special districts where fraud can occur.

Average Life of a Fraud

In the beginning of my career, I naively believed that fraud was instantaneously detected as it occurred—surely within a month's time. But the ACFE's fraud survey consistently shows that frauds have a life of about eighteen months before detection. Bear in mind this statistic reflects fraud cases where theft has been detected; unknown frauds are not included in the computation. Some local government frauds exist for decades without detection.

Fraud—Where It Happens

The 2012 ACFE's *Report to the Nations* found that governments are the second most commonly victimized industry (trailing only banking and financial services). And within governments, the 2012 survey reflects the following concentrations of fraud schemes:[1]

Scheme	Percent of Cases
Corruption	35.5%
Billing	23.4%
Noncash	19.1%
Skimming	17.7%
Expense Reimbursement	13.5%
Payroll	12.8%

1   Note: Some fraud cases include more than one scheme.

Check Tampering	10.6%
Cash on Hand	8.5%
Cash Larceny	7.1%
Financial Statement Fraud	6.4%
Register Disbursement	2.8%

In the following pages, we will focus on the areas that open the door to the greatest potential damage in your government. Expense reimbursement fraud, for example, is common but usually involves less dollar damage than corruption. So we will spend more time examining corruption and other areas where the threat of loss is greatest.

Stealing From Little Old Ladies

Many who steal from local governments view their theft as taking from the government itself. But from whom is the fraudster ultimately stealing? The local citizens—from Mr. Johnson, the owner of the local feed and seed; Mrs. Durham, the pastor's wife; Lloyd Tailor, a cotton farmer; and Rez Jacobs, the postmaster. These people pay property taxes, water fees, and all the other sources of money that flow into the local government. The fraudster is stealing from his next door neighbor, from those he goes to church with, from members of the local Lions Club, and from volunteer firefighters.

Those who steal from local governments tell themselves things like, "The city doesn't need this money, and besides, it's *the government*." Stealing, at least psychologically, is easier if the thief sees himself as taking from a cold sterile entity rather than from his neighbors. Taking from *the government* is easier than pilfering from the little old ladies down at the local senior citizens' center, though this is exactly what is occurring. You may, at this point, be thinking, "Only callous people would do such a thing." Well, let's see.

Stealing While Dying

In one of the strangest frauds I've seen, the bookkeeper was stealing money while dying. Going to meet your Maker with the fresh scent of theft on your hands is not a good way to go.

I had provided external audit services to this health department for years and knew the bookkeeper (we'll call her Katie) quite well. She sent me thank you cards—yes, thank you cards—for my audit work. Katie was polite, well spoken, and great at her job. If ever I thought there was someone who would not (and could not) steal, it was—you guessed it—Katie.

But external circumstances can make even the best people do the improbable. During the course of one audit year, Katie developed cancer. The medical treatments resulted in numerous medical bills, many of which she received while still working off and on. Sadly, she eventually died.

Knowing that Katie had passed away, I knew the audit would be challenging, especially since the health department board had not hired anyone to replace her. Upon my arrival I requested the bank statements, but the remaining employees could not locate them (not a good sign). I thought maybe she had taken the bank statements home and had not returned them due to her illness. Her family members said no. After the employees had searched for some time with no result, the health department requisitioned the bank statements and cleared checks from the bank.

In reviewing the cleared checks, I quickly noticed round-dollar vendor checks written to Katie. The first one was for $7,000. My first thought was, "Not Katie. I've known her too long. No way. Surely an explanation exists." But there was another, and another...

Reporting the theft to the health department board was difficult. Here was an honest person who had stolen money because she felt she had to.

This is one case where I *wanted* to just let it go, to walk away and pretend it didn't happen. But I knew that was not an option. Can you imagine being the board member that called Katie's husband—just months after her death—and informed him of the theft? Fraud is an ugly thing.

If you're an auditor and you need a reason to communicate internal control weaknesses in an open manner, here's one—for the employee's own safety (not to mention your own). Sometimes money is too tempting, even for the best of people.

The Fraud Triangle

Fraud experts commonly explain fraud using the three elements of the fraud triangle:

1. Rationalization (Katie's unselfish desire to leave her family with no medical bills)
2. Incentive (need for cash to pay medical bills)
3. Opportunity (almost no segregation of duties)

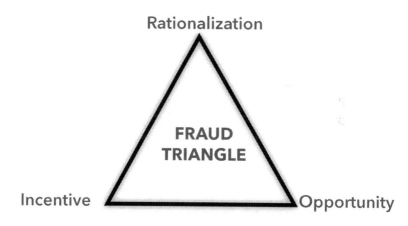

Katie was authorized to sign checks. Though the checks required two signatures, the bank cleared the checks with just Katie's signature. Since Katie keyed all transactions into the computer and reconciled the bank statements, she had the keys to the castle. We call this *opportunity*.

The people you're auditing are too honest to steal? Maybe. Or possibly you've worked side by side with governmental employees and you believe them to be saints. Maybe. We don't know about their personal lives—or what will happen in the future. Fraud percolates in these unshareable problem areas such as financial stress, gambling debts, affairs, or simply a desire to keep up with the Joneses. When it comes to designing accounting systems, we need to largely disregard the character of people working in the government and design the system as if fraud may happen.

Lessons Learned

- When records go missing—pay attention
- When you see round-dollar vendor checks—dig deeper
- When your government lacks segregation of duties—raise your antenna

While all three elements of the fraud triangle are important, in the following pages we will focus primarily upon opportunity. Of the three, opportunity is the part we can, at least to some degree, control. Governments are seldom able to manage a fraudster's incentive or rationalization. Incentive usually develops independent of the fraudster's employment; think of the medical bills, for example. The fraudster, prompted by the incentive, first calms his conscience by rationalizing. Next he exploits the opportunity (control weakness). If we can close the door to opportunity, fraud will be greatly diminished and possibly eliminated.

CHAPTER 2

General Local Government Fraud Prevention

Obviously fraud is alive and well in local governments. So how can we prevent it or at least mitigate it? First, we'll examine general fraud prevention controls (this chapter), before drilling down to prevention at the transaction cycle level (the next chapter).

This general controls section includes:
- Segregation of Duties
- A Simple Segregation of Duties Test
- Whistleblower Programs
- Red Flags of Fraud
- Hiring a Fraud Specialist—*Before* Fraud Occurs

Before we begin, let's put to rest three key misunderstandings; two about internal controls and one about outside audits.

First, local government external auditors are *not* responsible for the government's internal controls. Furthermore, if your external auditors develop your internal control structure, they are not independent and may not be able to perform your audit. They can and should make suggestions about controls, but they cannot design your entire internal control system. Ultimately, the development of a healthy internal control structure is the responsibility of the government. Yes, your government can contract for outside assistance in developing its internal control structure, but that help should not come from your external auditor. Second, sound internal controls will not eliminate *all* fraud. Even the best accounting system can be exploited.

What's the misunderstanding about external audits? Many governmental professionals and laypeople alike believe a clean audit opinion means the government has no fraud concerns—past or future. This belief is incorrect. Your external auditors gain an understanding of key transaction cycles *in order to plan the audit* but not for the purpose of fully vetting your internal controls.

As we will see later in the book, most external auditors—by design—are not even looking for immaterial fraud (though *immaterial* can mean thousands of dollars). Your auditor's definition and your definition of what is material (and what is not) may be completely different, especially if you are an elected official or government administrator.

An auditor may define materiality as $75,000 and your definition may be $100—like the difference in Venus and Mars, huh? So your auditor, by design, may not look for frauds involving $10,000, $20,000, or even more.

When a local government is audited, I find that the officials often think, "I've met my fiduciary and legal requirements. I'm done." It's as if this one step—an audit—provides immunity when fraud occurs. The prudent governmental administrator or elected official thinks differently. Audits are a wise tool. They are of great worth. But even so, they are not a cure-all. More needs to be done to protect the government, such as developing appropriate segregation of duties.

Segregation of Duties

Segregation of duties, an oft-cited prevention measure, is one of the most effective means to protect your government. There are, however, challenges to achieving appropriate control design, namely:

- Not many people understand how to design accounting systems.
- In small governments, fewer people are employed, making it more challenging to segregate duties.

Some twenty years ago I encountered my first local government fraud. Working as an external auditor for a mid-Georgia CPA firm, I was performing an audit of a county tax office. In my then short career, I had not seen accounting records so difficult to follow: bank reconciliations not performed, receipt books not agreeing with daily deposits, and several instances of the tax digest stamped "Paid" but there were no matching receipts. We mistook the first signs of fraud as sloppiness. After all, the tax commissioner was a young, seemingly innocent lady with a pleasant demeanor. But as we dug deeper, it became apparent that more was amiss than the bookkeeping, and before it was over, the FBI and the IRS were involved. The small county had lost over $500,000. How? The tax commissioner had control of all facets of the accounting process.

Weak segregation of duties opens the door of opportunity, enabling the fraudster to steal and conceal. Opportunity manifests itself when one person is allowed to perform more than one of the following duties:

1. Custody of assets
2. Reconciliations
3. Authorization
4. Bookkeeping[2]

The tax commissioner performed multiple functions. She sent tax bills, collected cash, recorded transactions, and reconciled the books (or at least had the responsibility for doing so).

If a government is too small to properly segregate duties, implement *compensating controls*—usually a second-person review of the activity, often performed by another official.

---

2   Note—The four elements can be remembered using the acrostic: CRAB.

If no one in the government is available to perform the second-person review, consider hiring an outside Certified Public Accountant or Certified Fraud Examiner to perform surprise tests of the accounting system. (See *Fraud Prevention for (Very) Small Governments* in the Supplemental Information section of this book for test suggestions.)

A Simple Segregation of Duties Test

When I review a transaction cycle (e.g., accounts payable/expenses), I always complete the following table:
1. Custody of Assets: Eldridge P. Johnson, III
2. Reconciliation: I. Cheatum
3. Authorization: I. Cheatum
4. Bookkeeping: Suzy Que

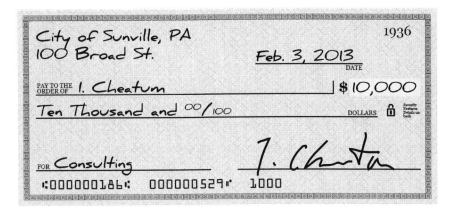

If one person's name appears more than once in the table, segregation of duties is lacking. For example, if I. Cheatum authorizes the transaction by signing checks, and he also reconciles the bank account, a segregation of duties weakness exists.

Use these same four attributes (authorization, bookkeeping, reconciliation, and custody of assets) in assessing the controls of any transaction cycle (e.g., receipting, disbursements, and payroll). Again, if one person performs two or more of the four elements, you have a segregation of duties issue that may require a compensating control, such as a second-person review.

I find that most people struggle with assessing a government's segregation of duties; consequently, they prefer a checklist to vet internal controls. While no checklist is foolproof, you'll find a document titled *Internal Control Checklist for Local Governments* in the Supplemental Information section of this book. This checklist will get you started in evaluating your government's internal controls.

Whistleblower Programs

"Well, he asked me for anything outside the ordinary routine."[3]

The most effective method of preventing and detecting fraud is to ask those associated with your government to report "anything outside the ordinary routine," though they will need anonymity in order to do so. Why the secrecy? You want those with pertinent information to be free from potential reprisals and from the possibility of looking foolish—reporting what looks like fraud, but is not.

Dollar for dollar, a sound whistleblower program is the most effective means of detecting and preventing fraud, more so than *anything* else you can do. The biennial ACFE *Report to the Nations* repeatedly reflects the effectiveness of whistleblower programs. And yet, you seldom see such a program in local governments. Why? Possibly, it's because governments rely too much on external audits. If true, it's a mistake, and I say this as a practicing external auditor. Believe it or not, a whistleblower program is much more effective in preventing or detecting fraud than external audits, and it costs much less. The 2012 ACFE *Report to the Nations* stated that whistleblower tips unveiled fraud in 43% of the survey results; by comparison, external audits unearthed fraud at a rate of only

---

3   *The Hound of the Baskervilles* by Sir Arthur Conan Doyle

3%. Let's suppose your annual external audit costs $40,000 and your whistleblower program, $4,000. Even so, your government is almost fifteen times more likely to detect fraud by a tip than by your annual audit.

Since fraud is detected at an extremely high rate by *tips*, make it easy for employees, elected officials, citizens, and vendors to communicate information. You can think of a whistleblower program as a type of radar, one that receives signals of fraud occurring in your government. For instance, an employee knows about the accounting director's illicit drug use; a vendor is asked to provide a kickback to the mayor; or an elected official sees an employee stealing equipment. Make it easy for these persons to communicate their inside knowledge, and the signals will come.

Should fraud tips be communicated internally or externally? I recommend you use an outside whistleblower company that provides a 1-800 phone number (called a hotline) and takes calls 24/7. Given that hotline employees are trained to solicit and document fraud-related information, you'll receive more transparent communications. In addition, since the whistleblower's voice will not be recognized, he'll feel safer. The result: more frequent sharing of fraud-related knowledge. The 2012 ACFE *Report to the Nations* found that "Organizations with some form of hotline in place saw a much higher likelihood that a fraud would be detected by a tip (51%) than organizations without such a hotline (35%)."

Once a hotline company is enlisted, it will, at a minimum, advertise the means by which your governmental employees, elected officials, citizens, and vendors can communicate information—usually a 1-800 phone number. The advertisements often include physical posters and postings to your government's websites, including intranets. In addition, some whistleblower companies will teach your employees the red flags of fraud so they'll know what to look for and what to communicate.

How does the hotline company transmit the information to your government? The company gathers and relays, at appointed times, the accumulated information to a designated person at your government. It's up to the designee of your government (or an assigned committee) to determine the next step.

A less common whistleblower provision—but one to strongly consider—is to offer monetary rewards for fraud-related tips. The ACFE found that rewards are offered in less than 10% of organizations. Such payments are often a percent of proven fraud damages (or the government may offer a flat-rate reward upon the corroboration of the fraud). Check with your legal counsel, however, prior to offering rewards.

Your employees will be better prepared to blow the whistle if they know what red flags to look for—the topic we'll now examine.

Red Flags of Fraud

Would your employees recognize fraud if it occurred? Are they aware of the signs of fraud? Some red flags are obvious. Others are not.

Here are some sample red flags that governmental employees and elected officials should look for:

External Red Flags

- Unexplained increases in the wealth of an accounting employee or elected official
- Employee personal problems such as a divorce, substance abuse, financial difficulties, legal problems
- Employee living beyond his or her means
- Unusually close employee association with a vendor

Cash Receipts and Billing Red Flags

- Taxpayer complaints concerning nonpayment notices (even though payment has been made)
- A pattern of customer complaints in the utility billing and collection process
- Substantial write-offs of receivables without support

- Unexplained decreases in revenues
- A pattern of missing receipt forms

Disbursements and Purchasing Red Flags

- Altered or incomplete supporting documentation for disbursements
- Purchasing party (e.g., department head) picking up processed vendor checks rather than accounts payable personnel mailing them
- Unexplained increases in expenses
- Excessive expenses when compared to the budget
- Vendors without physical addresses

Payroll Red Flags

- Employees with no or little payroll deductions
- Excessive overtime expenses
- Excessive payroll expenses when compared to the budget

Capital Assets Red Flags

- Winning bid appears too high; all contractors submit consistently high bids
- Qualified construction contractors not submitting bids
- Reports of missing capital assets
- A lack of accountability for capital assets

General Red Flags

- A refusal by accounting personnel to take vacations
- Unwillingness to share accounting duties
- Employee irritability or defensiveness
- Complaints about inadequate employee pay
- A lack of transparency in accounting
- Rumors of unethical conduct
- A history of corruption in the government
- Financial decisions made by one person with little or no accountability

- Undocumented journal entries
- Untimely bank reconciliations
- Inexperienced or lax accounting personnel
- Missing accounting records

Just because a red flag exists does not mean that fraud has occurred, but these are the types of signs that employees and elected officials should be aware of. It certainly wouldn't hurt to periodically provide your personnel with basic fraud training so they'll know what these signs are.

Often, governments hire a fraud prevention specialist after fraud is discovered, but as we will now see, hiring an experienced fraud examiner early is better than later.

Hiring a Fraud Specialist—*Before* Fraud Occurs

Sometimes external audits detect fraud, but they are not a silver bullet. (According to the ACFE, external audits detect fraud less than 10% of the time.) While audit standards require auditors to perform limited reviews of accounting systems and internal controls, they do not require a review of *all* accounting functions, and normally, auditors do not provide assurances about these controls.

If it's not the job of the external auditor to detect all fraud, whose responsibility is it? Detection of fraud lies primarily with the government. Think of this issue in terms of who should prevent theft from a home. Should it be the homeowner or the police? If the homeowner puts no locks on the doors and leaves the windows open, who is at fault when theft occurs? Even though the police are crime detection and prevention professionals, the primary responsibility lies with the homeowner. So how can a local government, especially one without trained fraud prevention personnel, address the potential for theft?

Consider contracting with a fraud prevention specialist to review your government's internal controls. Have this trained professional (preferably a person with fraud credentials and experience in local governments) review your accounting system and report any internal control weaknesses to your accounting department and governing board. But who should hire the fraud professional?

To avoid a situation where a potential fraudster (e.g., finance director) is hiring the fraud prevention specialist, it is best for the governing body and the government's accounting management to make this decision together. Once hired, the fraud specialist should report to the government's governing body and financial management. I once encountered a situation where the person committing the fraud was instrumental in hiring me for external audit purposes. After initial fraud evidence was discovered, this same person threatened to fire me (and actually did when I refused to compromise).

The fraud prevention specialist should perform two primary functions:
1. Map the accounting system and internal controls
2. Perform periodic surprise audits

First, have the fraud prevention professional map your internal controls and provide written reports explaining your accounting system's strengths and weaknesses.

What is mapping? Think of it as connecting the dots. Control weaknesses become apparent as we connect the dots of your accounting system (with words and flowcharts). As your government grows in size, mapping becomes more important. Given that accounting systems evolve over time, rather than by a planned design, control weaknesses may develop without anyone's knowledge. We may believe we understand an accounting system, but without a map, do we? (Ask yourself, "Does any single person in the government understand all the accounting processes?" Often the answer is no. Neither do many external auditors.)

Second, your fraud prevention professional can make periodic surprise unannounced visits—focusing on any identified control weaknesses. I usually advise governments to announce the coming surprise visits—not the dates or areas to be examined, just that the visits are forthcoming. Why? To prevent employees from saying "I'm being picked on." Rotate and vary the areas being reviewed. This keeps everyone honest.

My last suggestion in hiring an outside fraud specialist is don't use your external audit firm. If your external audit team provides internal audit services, the question may arise, "Are the external auditors independent?" In other words, can they audit their own work and be impartial? It's doubtful. Consequently, hiring a fraud specialist not associated with your external audit firm is advisable.

You may be wondering, "How much would it cost to hire a fraud prevention specialist?" It depends mainly on what you ask this person to do. Fraud prevention work can be tailored to a budget. Of course, the smaller the budget, the fewer the services offered. If your government can't afford the cost of hiring a fraud specialist, are there any alternatives? The answer is yes. Your government can perform self-audit procedures. For suggestions, see *Fraud Prevention for (Very) Small Governments* in the Supplemental Information section of this book.

CHAPTER 3

Transaction Level Fraud Prevention

We've reviewed general fraud controls. Now it's time to dig a little deeper, down where the action really happens—at the transaction level.

Once while hiking in north Georgia, I walked around a curve—and there standing before me were three bears (Goldilocks was nowhere to be seen). I didn't know whether to run, scream, or just stand still. So I did all three—I think. You may respond the same way as we make the turn toward transaction level fraud. But you'll soon feel better. I promise. We'll examine how fraud affects the following transaction cycles:

- Cash Receipts and Billing
- Disbursement and Purchasing
- Payroll
- Capital Assets

Misappropriation of assets commonly occurs in governments as money comes in and as money goes out. Since cash is often stolen as money comes in, we'll examine how cash is receipted. In the disbursements and payroll chapters to follow, we'll see how funds are stolen as money goes out. Finally, we'll close our transaction level discussion by seeing how capital assets are stolen by physical theft and how capital asset costs are inflated through corruption.

———

CASH RECEIPTS AND BILLING FRAUD

Whenever I'm teaching fraud classes, I often hold up a $20 bill in the air and place it on the table. Then I say: "I'm going to leave this $20 bill on the table for the night. Tomorrow morning I will return. Which do you think is most likely to be here? The $20, or the table?" Everyone laughs. They get my point: Cash is liquid, moveable, and does not require conversion.

We'll now explore four areas where theft of cash often occurs in governments:

- Decentralized Cash Collections
- Cash Drawers
- Elected Officials and Collections
- Check-for-Cash Substitution

Decentralized Cash Collections

How many times have you seen a local newspaper article with news like the following?

> *Johnson County's longtime court clerk admitted today to stealing $120,000 of court funds from 2006 through 2009. Joan Cook, 62, faces up to 10 years in federal prison after pleading guilty to federal tax evasion.*

Sometimes the causes of such cash thefts are (1) decentralized collection points and (2) a lack of accounting controls.

Governments commonly have several collection points. Examples include:

- Recreation department

- Police department
- Development authority
- Water and sewer department
- Airport authority
- Landfill
- Building and code enforcement
- Courts

Many governments have more than a dozen receipting locations. With cash flowing in so many places, it's no wonder that cash theft is common. Each cash receipt area may have different accounting procedures—some with physical receipt books, some with computerized receipting, and some with no receipting system at all. Often, these decentralized cash collections points funnel into a central location (e.g., county administrative office).

A more centralized receipting system reduces the possibility of theft, but many governments may not be able to centralize the receipting function.

Why?

- Elected officials, such as tax commissioners, often determine how monies are collected without input from the final receiving government (e.g., county commissioners or school). Consequently, each elected official may decide to use a different receipting system.
- Customer convenience may also drive the receipting location as in the case of senior citizen centers.
- Other locations, such as landfills, are purposely placed on the outer boundary of the government's geographic area.

The result: Widely differing receipting systems. Numerous receipting locations with varying controls lead to a higher risk of theft.

If cash collections are not receipted, it's more likely that cash will be stolen. If the transaction is recorded, the receipt record must be altered, destroyed, or hidden to cover up the theft. That's why *it's critical to capture the transaction as early as possible*. Doing so makes theft more difficult to hide.

If segregation of duties is not possible, consider having a second person review the activity—either an employee of the government or maybe an outside consultant.

Cash Drawers

Each cash drawer should be assigned to a single person. If theft occurs and multiple people work from one cash drawer, you may not be able to determine which person took the funds. Each cash drawer should have a base amount at the beginning of the day—for example, $500. Once the drawer is settled at the end of the day, the $500 will be retained in the cash drawer.

All payments collected during a day should be reconciled to the receipts issued. These days, those receipts will most often be computer-generated, though some governments still use manual receipt books. Whether using a computer or manual system, all receipts should be accounted for. Be mindful that a second receipt book can spell theft when physical receipt books are used. Here's an example.

A police chief in one small Georgia city had two ticket receipt books, one for *checks* received and one for *cash* received. The chief would deposit all checks to an appropriate bank account but would pocket the cash, receipting these monies with the second receipt book and marking the related tickets "Paid." The theft was detected by the external auditors as they noticed a significant decrease in fine money while performing a trend analysis. When the chief was questioned, he openly confessed to the scheme.

The normal accounting procedures for a cash drawer activity are as follows:

1. Collect and receipt funds collected; restrictively endorse checks
2. Only one person works each cash drawer
3. At the end of the day or shift, the person working the drawer:
   a. Adds all cash and checks received
   b. Prints the receipt summary from the computer or adds the physical receipts
   c. Reconciles payments received to the summary of receipts
   d. Cash drawer operator initials the summary of receipts noting any differences
4. Person operating the cash drawer provides the payments received and the summary of receipts to a supervisor who recounts the cash collected and reconciles it to the summary of receipts. The supervisor initials the summary of receipts as evidence of the review.
5. Supervisor creates a deposit slip and notes the amount of cash and checks being deposited
6. Deposit is made by a third person who receives a validated deposit ticket from the bank, returning the deposit ticket to the supervisor for reconciliation to the deposit slip
7. Computer cash receipts are processed, causing the general ledger to be updated (or physical receipts are entered)

Variations of this basic framework are numerous. So consider whether adequate segregation of duties exists. Often, the person receipting cash will also enter the transaction into the receipting system. Since you normally desire to segregate receipting (custody of cash) from keying (entering information into the accounting system), is this okay? That's where the supervisor's review comes into the picture. This review ensures that the entries made are appropriate—even though one person handled the cash and keyed in the transaction.

While the supervisor does not enter the receipt, he or she will review the entries, usually before the receipts are posted to the general ledger.

The government should have a policy in place that disallows the cashing of personal checks. It's too easy for loans to be made from a cash drawer. How? The loan takes the form of a cashed personal check in the drawer. For example, the person writes a personal check for $1,000 and takes that amount of cash from the drawer; the check is left in the drawer each day until the money can be returned. Of course, if a supervisor reviews the daily activity, then it is improbable that this scheme would be attempted. But, if daily activity is not reviewed by the supervisor, such an unapproved loan can easily occur without detection. And we know that once such a scheme works for a little while, the amount of the loan will often increase over time because the fraudster feels emboldened by prior success.

Elected Officials and Collections

Elected officials often have sole discretion over their departments. Consequently, the accounting processes will be dictated by the officeholder who may have no prior experience with accounting, especially if he or she is serving for the first time. As a result, the public servant may not understand the purpose of segregating accounting duties or the importance of depositing and remitting funds on a timely basis. Even if state or local laws require the remittance of collected funds within a certain time frame, the official may not be aware of those laws and will sometimes even ignore them.

For instance, a tax commissioner may be required to remit monies collected every two weeks to the county commissioners' office. If the property taxes are not remitted on a timely basis, the county may lack sufficient funds to pay bills and meet payroll. From a fraud perspective, the tax commissioner's decision to hold on to funds creates additional opportunities for theft; you can steal only what is present. So timely remittances of funds are important. As the new external auditor for a county, I once entered a tax commissioner's office and saw cash covering her entire desktop. So I remarked to her, "You haven't made a deposit in while?" She laughed and said, "Yeah, I've been too busy lately." We later learned she had stolen several hundred thousand dollars.

Elected officials may believe they can do as they wish, and they sometimes do. The tax commissioner mentioned above was required by state law to remit funds to the county commissioners' office once every two weeks. Even after the commissioners' office demanded she comply, she ignored their request for several months.

Elected constitutional officers may believe, "I was elected by the people, so I am not accountable to anyone else." These very words have been spoken to me. It's as if the official is saying, "Hey auditor, you have no right to question me." Sometimes this is just pride and sometimes it's a cover for theft. You never know which—until it's too late. This I do know: My antennae go up when I hear it. I'm more prone to push when I see an elected official or administrative person posture in this manner. Why *hide anything* unless *there is something to hide*?

This can get challenging, especially when the elected official has power (as in the power to fire the auditor). I once found an illegal act committed by a county commissioner. When I explained to him that the illegality would be reported, he told me in no uncertain terms, that "I will find another auditor if you don't leave me alone." I knew he had the power to deliver. My response was, "You do what you have to do, and I'll do what I have to do." I reported the illegal act and was soon informed that I was no longer the auditor. These struggles can get ugly and costly, so be prepared. He is still in office, and I am not the auditor. But I sleep well, thank you.

Check-for-Cash Substitution

Sometimes employees steal rebate or refund checks and convert them to cash for personal use. How can an employee convert a check made out to the government to cash?

Let's say Bill Johnson opens the mail for a city. One envelope contains a rebate check for $3,314.15. He knows from experience that the city annually receives dozens of such rebate checks, and he recently heard the finance director say, "I'm in the dark about the rebate checks." Bill steals the check, but he has a problem. He needs to convert the check to cash.

Bill also works one of the city's cash drawers which often has over $10,000 (in cash and checks) at the end of the day. Bill, while no one is looking, places the $3,314.15 check in the cash drawer and removes the same amount of cash. The $3,314.15 check is made out to the city, just like other checks he's collected, so no one will notice anything unusual. And since his *total* of cash and checks still equals his daily receipts summary, his supervisor does not detect the check-for-cash substitution. Mission accomplished. So how do we prevent check-for-cash fraud?

Preventing this type of fraud is simple—just require the cash drawer operator to record on each receipt the amount of cash or check payment received. (A copy of the receipt is given to the customer.) Then, at the end of the day, reconcile the daily amount of cash and checks from the cash drawer to the daily receipts summary, which should have (1) a total for cash and (2) a total for checks. You will know something is wrong if the composition of cash and checks (per the daily receipt report) does not agree with the actual cash and checks received. The daily receipt summary should be attached to the cash and checks given to the supervisor who will review the cash drawer report and complete the deposit slip.

Many small governments have one person opening the mail, receipting payments, making deposits, and recording the related accounting entries—this is a recipe for fraud.

In such circumstances, other preventive measures may be needed, such as the one that follows.

After requiring cash or check notations on each receipt, consider periodically performing surprise test counts—in the middle of the day—of cash and check collections. Have your internal or external auditors perform these surprise audits. If this procedure is implemented, tell your accounting personnel beforehand that their work is subject to random surprise tests. This keeps them honest.

In a twist of the check-for-cash substitution scheme, cash receipting personnel may steal ("borrow") cash by placing a personal check or an I.O.U. in the cash drawer and taking an equal amount of cash. The clerk might simply write on an index card "I.O.U. $400—Bill Johnson" and take that amount of money.

DISBURSEMENT AND PURCHASING FRAUD

As we make a turn to disbursements and purchasing fraud, you'll see there are a multitude of ways funds can be stolen.

All of the fraud surveys that I've seen identify corruption and misappropriation of assets as primary methods of stealing from governments. Though the disbursement cycle can be exploited in many ways, we will focus on:

- Bribes
- Fictitious Vendors
- Misuse of Old Vendors
- Misuse of Existing Vendors
- Altering Check Payees
- Duplicate Payments to Valid Vendors
- Credit Cards
- Wire Transfers

To simplify your understanding of disbursement fraud, remember that monies are primarily stolen with:
1. Checks
2. Electronic Payments
3. Debit/Credit Cards
4. Bribes or Kickbacks (Corruption)

The first three categories are usually internal threats, while corruption is an external threat. The first three involve the theft of cash from the government, while the fourth uses a more indirect method—the vendor inflates the price of goods sold to the government to recoup the cost of the bribe. First we will examine bribery.

Bribes

"A bribe is seen as a charm by the one who gives it; they think success will come at every turn."[4]

The FBI performed a sting operation involving two Georgia city council members. The Bureau's court complaint alleged that two city council members contacted a city vendor requesting a bribe. The vendor, according to the complaint, had previously provided services to the city, but when the contract came up for renewal, the city officials sought monetary encouragement (also known as cash) to continue the arrangement.

The vendor's president, once aware of the proposed bribe, contacted the FBI which in turn conducted a sting operation. On an arranged date, the vendor's CFO delivered $20,000 in cash to one of the city council members; meanwhile, the conversation between the CFO and the council member was recorded. Soon thereafter, arrests were made.

Once, early in my career, I noticed that chemical purchases in a city sewer department had doubled. Upon investigation,

4 Proverbs 17:8 NIV

it was found that the chemical sales representative was bribing the department head with boxes of liquor. The greater the chemical purchases, the more the liquor flowed.

In these two examples, the cash and the liquor were paid for by outside companies. If bribes are paid for by outside companies, how do they harm governments?

How Are Governments Harmed?

Bribes harm organizations *indirectly*. Vendors usually don't absorb the cost of the bribe; they pass the expense along to the government in the form of increased invoice billings, or the vendor will, in some cases, provide substandard products or services. Either way, the government loses and the person receiving the bribe walks away with cash or a free vacation or a free car or ... well, you get the picture.

So how common is corruption? Very. The ACFE's 2012 *Report to the Nations* disclosed corruption was the root of 35% of all government fraud. Given the frequency of corruption, auditors need to understand who can harm the government—those with the power to buy.

The Power to Buy

Auditors need to remember that bribes are directed at those who have the power to buy. That person can be an elected official, a purchasing agent, or anyone else who can authorize a disbursement. Many times, in small governments, that power rests with department heads and elected officials. Sports tickets, cash, vacations, and sexual favors are just a few of the bribes offered, but know this: The vendor will exploit the purchaser's weaknesses—whatever those are.

Sometimes the gifts are provided after purchases are made as an incentive for the decision maker to buy more. Other times payments are made prior to the purchase. Payments made prior to a purchase are considered *bribes*; payments made afterwards, *gratuities*. Either way, the intent is the same: Get the purchaser to buy something that is not needed. Once the purchaser is hooked, it's difficult to stop. He rationalizes, "I've previously accepted payments so I can't do any *more* harm to myself. I'll just continue the ride."

Every local government needs to spell out what gifts are acceptable or if gifts are allowed at all. It's one thing for a vendor to send a box of chocolates at Christmas; it's an entirely different thing for that same vendor to send your purchasing agent to Las Vegas.

Detecting Bribes

These bribery cases remind me that uncovering corruption is demanding and that detection normally involves:
- A tip (usually from someone within the organization)
- Assistance from law enforcement

The ACFE's biennial fraud survey indicates that over 60% of corruption-related frauds are unearthed by tips or by accident. Audit procedures, however, can be used to detect corruption, such as comparing individual vendor costs over a period of time. I suggest this test be performed and advertised (let everyone know) so that those tempted will think twice— the potential of detection is a strong deterrent.

How?
1. Obtain the check register for multiple periods (e.g., three years).
2. Sort the payments by vendor name, aggregate the total paid by vendor and period.
3. Compare the periodic vendor totals (e.g., annual vendor totals for each of the three years).
4. Investigate unusual differences.

Inflated invoices are a smoking gun. If you note unexplained increases, determine who approved the purchases.

Also inquire within departments about faulty or substandard products received (another smoking gun); then, if significant, see who approved the related purchases, especially if the deficient product is repeatedly received.

Mitigating Corruption

To mitigate corruption, implement these controls:
- For significant purchases, require sealed bids that are opened in the presence of multiple people; the government should establish a dollar threshold for which sealed bids are required.
- Implement a whistleblower program (include vendors).
- Require periodic vendor audits (let your elected officials and employees know this will occur); consider providing results to your elected body as a whole.
- Implement a conflict of interest policy.
- Implement a bribery prevention policy (include gifts).
- For significant construction contracts, monitor all phases of the project, including solicitation of bids, awarding of the bid, development of the contract, on-site construction and related billing, and contract change orders. Consider hiring a second party—someone other than the contractor and someone who fully understands construction—to monitor all phases of the project.

Keep in mind that corruption is more likely to occur for *complex large dollar purchases* such as construction projects. The magnitude of the purchase price and complexity of the project make it easier to hide the kickback expense. In other words, a government is more likely to pay for inflated invoices without questioning when it does not understand the details of what it is paying for.

Fictitious Vendors

Fictitious vendor fraud can be an insidious threat to a local government. This theft is usually committed by a person with the ability to establish new vendors in the accounting system (often the accounts payable clerk). If you are going to prevent this fraud, you need to know how it works.

First, the clerk creates the fictitious vendor in the accounts payable system using his own address (or that of an accomplice); alternatively, he may use a personal P.O. box (which is more common). Second, the clerk creates fictitious vendor invoices to support the payments; often, these invoices are for *services* rather than for a *physical product*. Since no shipped asset will be received by the government, it's easier to conceal the fraud. Finally, the accounts payable clerk issues the vendor checks; since the fictitious vendor check address is that of the accounting clerk, it is mailed directly to the fraudster (or his accomplice). Here's an example.

John, the accounts payable clerk, sets up the fictitious vendor, Rutland Consulting, and keys *his* (John's) address (P.O. Box 798, Atlanta, Georgia, 99890) into the vendor master file. To save time, the city has elected to have all checks signed electronically by the computerized system, so printed checks have signatures on them, and it just so happens that John prints all checks. John records an accounts payable amount of $3,322 to Rutland Consulting. To conceal the fraud, John creates a fictitious consulting services invoice from Rutland Consulting (especially designed for the auditors), and he codes the expense to an account which has plenty of remaining budgetary appropriation. Now John prints and mails the checks (including the fictitious vendor check). Two days later, voilà, John picks up his check at his P.O. box. John has opened a bank account for—you guessed it—Rutland Consulting; he is the only authorized check signer for the account. After depositing the city-issued check to the Rutland Consulting checking account, he writes checks to himself. Soon John's friends are impressed with his shiny new bass boat.

While reading about John's fraud, you may have been thinking, "Not a problem in my government. Our checks are physically signed." Consider, however, that signed checks can be created by:

- Forging signatures on manual checks
- Signing checks with signature stamps

The fraudster might also, in another twist to this scheme, just wire the money electronically. If the fraudster can create a signed check or wire funds, then the fictitious vendor scheme becomes a possibility.

Banks generally do not visually inspect checks as they clear (how could they, given the volume of daily checks?), so a forged signature will usually suffice. John's theft described above becomes easier if he also reconciles the related bank statement—no second pair of eyes will inspect the cleared checks.

City or county department heads can also use a fictitious vendor scheme if they can submit believable new-vendor documentation. Many governments do not verify the existence of new vendors; therefore, a department head can merely send a false invoice to the payables clerk and receive payment. Oftentimes when an accounts payable clerk receives an invoice, he will add the new vendor to the accounts payable master file without verifying that the vendor is real. Since department heads often code and approve invoices (by writing the expense account number on the invoice and initialing the same), the payment will be recorded in an account of the department head's choice. Again, such invoices are usually for *services* (e.g., electrical repair)—that way, the accounts payable department is not waiting for receiving documents (e.g., packing slips) before payment is made.

The fictitious vendor fraud hinges on three factors:

1. Getting the fictitious vendor added to the accounts payable vendor list (along with the false address)
2. Getting the payment made (either by controlling the whole payment process or by having the authority to approve disbursements)
3. Getting the payment posted to an account where its presence goes unnoticed

If appropriate segregation of duties does not exist, or if someone has the power to add new vendors and to authorize payments, the fictitious vendor fraud becomes a possibility.

Mitigating Fictitious Vendor Risk

To mitigate the risk of fictitious vendors, do the following:
- Require vendors to provide a physical address (even if payments are to be mailed to a P.O. box).
- Require the accounts payable clerk to verify the existence of the new vendor (by calling the vendor or Googling the vendor's address).
- Segregate duties (namely the ability to add new vendors and the power to authorize check payments).
- Periodically review and purge vendor files.

Misuse of Old Vendors

If an accounting clerk can't add fictitious vendors without raising red flags, he can use an old vendor to accomplish the same goal. The accounting clerk finds a vendor for which the government has made no recent payments. Next, in the master vendor file, he changes the address of the old vendor to his own address. Thereafter, he follows the previously described fictitious-vendor-scheme steps, submitting a fictitious invoice in the name of the old vendor, and receiving the vendor check in his mailbox. The fraudster opens a bank account in the name of the old vendor and deposits the fraudulent checks. Again, the fraudster is the only authorized check signer for the bank account.

Can you see why it's important to limit who can add vendors or change addresses in the accounts payable system? Many small governments provide open access to all users of the accounting system (for example, the receipting clerk has access to the accounts payable module); so if an employee has access to the accounts payable module and that person understands how the payable system works, this type of theft is possible. Check with your software company (or IT person) to see if the access rights are appropriately assigned; in computer-speak, this assignment process is called logical access. Not appropriately assigning computer access rights is equivalent to leaving the cookie jar unguarded—anyone can take a bite.

Misuse of Existing Vendors

Some accounting clerks steal by temporarily changing the address of an existing vendor for one or two payments. The accounting clerk submits a fictitious invoice for a real vendor, changes the address of the real vendor to his own, and processes payables as usual. The check is conveniently delivered to the home of the accounting clerk. As soon as the checks are cut, the accounting clerk changes the address back to the vendor's true address. This type of theft is easier to commit if the government commonly makes several payments to this real vendor; adding one or two payments will often not raise a red flag.

Altering Check Payees

As a kid I once threw a match into a half-gallon of gasoline just to see what would happen. I quickly found out. In a panic, I kicked the gas container—a plastic milk jug—several times, thinking this would somehow put the fire out. But just the opposite occurred, and when my father found out, something else was on fire.

Some accounting weaknesses create unintended consequences. Show me an accounting clerk who (1) signs checks [whether by hand, with a signature stamp, or with a computer-generated signature], (2) posts transactions to the accounting system, and (3) reconciles the bank statements, and I will show you another combustible situation.

Here's how one city clerk created her own blaze. Using the city's signature stamp, the clerk signed handwritten checks made out to herself; however, when the payee name was entered into the general ledger (with a journal entry), another name was used—that of a legitimate vendor.

For example, Susie, the clerk, created manual checks made out to herself and signed them with the signature stamp. But the check payee was entered into the accounting system as Macon Hardware. In addition, she allocated the disbursements to accounts with sufficient remaining budgetary balances. The subterfuge worked since the expense accounts reflected appropriate vendor activity and expenses stayed within the budgetary appropriations. No red flags.

The accounting clerk, when confronted with evidence of her deception, responded, "I don't know why I did it, I didn't need the money." We do a disservice to accounting employees when we make it so easy to steal. Given human nature, we should do what we can to limit the temptation.

How?

First, if possible, segregate the disbursement duties so that only one person performs each of the following:

- Creating checks
- Signing checks
- Reconciling bank statements
- Entering checks into the general ledger

If you can't segregate duties, have someone (the mayor, a nonaccounting employee, or an outside CPA) review cleared checks for appropriateness.

Second, have another person approve all journal entries. False journal entries can be used to hide theft.

Third, limit access to check stock. It's usually wise to keep blank check stock locked up until needed.

Finally, limit who can sign checks, and deep-six the signature stamp.

External auditors should consider testing a random sample of cleared checks by agreeing them to related invoices. In other words, work from the cleared check to the invoice. The auditor should pull the invoices from the invoice file. If the check payee has been altered, you will normally not find a corresponding invoice. Pay particular attention to checks with payees who are employees of the government.

Duplicate Payments to Valid Vendors

Why should accounts payable clerks stamp invoices as *"Paid"* upon payment?

- So the invoice is not *accidentally* paid twice
- So the invoice is not *purposefully* used by the accounting clerk to trick the check signer into signing a second check for the same invoice

This second check can be stolen by the accounting clerk and converted to cash (by manipulating the endorsement or by opening a bank account in the name of the vendor).

Suppose your government provides all invoices to the mayor for inspection. After inspecting the invoices, she signs the related checks. Since the accounting clerk did not mark the invoice *"Paid,"* the clerk can present the same invoice to the mayor a second time (a few weeks later). Once the check is signed, the fraudster can steal the second payment.

In another twist on this scheme, the accounting clerk purposefully mails the second check to the valid vendor, making a double-payment on purpose. Then the clerk calls the vendor saying, "I made a mistake and paid you twice. Would you please mail the refund check to me?" Once the refund check is received, the fraudster converts the check to cash.

Credit Cards

Many smaller governments have three or four credit cards. Often these cards are kept in someone's unlocked desk drawer and everyone in the office knows where they are. In these same governments, no card usage policy exists. It's as if everyone is told, "If you need to bypass the purchasing policy, here's the way to do it."

Here are a few recommendations for the use of credit cards:

1. Limit the number of cards issued.
2. Assign each card to *one* person.
3. Set up a relatively low credit limit for each card.
4. Keep all cards in a secure location.
5. Restrict card usage to particular vendors.
6. Require the person to provide support for each purchase.
7. Reconcile monthly credit card statements to supporting documentation (provided by the card user). The person performing the reconciliation should not be the authorized card user. The person performing the reconciliation should provide details of any undocumented expenses to the finance director or an elected official.
8. If appropriate support is not provided, disallow the use of the credit card in the future and require the employee to reimburse the government.
9. Discontinue cards for terminated employees as soon as possible.
10. Consider not issuing credit cards. Instead, ask employees to use their personal credit cards and periodically file for reimbursement of expenses.

Wire Transfer Fraud

In one of the easiest thefts I've read about, a nonprofit administrative officer wired $6.9 million from an Ohio bank account to another account in Austria. The wire transfer originated with the fax of a letter which probably took less than an hour to create. Since the officer was authorized to make wire transfers, no one at the bank questioned the transaction—until it was too late. The fraudster landed in Austria, called his wife and said, "I'm not coming home." Interestingly, the wife called the police and turned her husband in. He later came back to the states of his own volition. He went to jail. I guess, after a few boat rides down the Danube, he missed his family.

It's easy for an accounting clerk or other authorized governmental official to wire funds and to cover his tracks with a journal entry—too easy in many cases. If an accountant or official has the ability to (1) wire funds by himself and (2) make journal entries without a second-person review, the government has left the fraud door wide open. Such a situation is not uncommon in governments.

As you think about wire transfers, consider that they originate with:

- Faxes
- Phone calls
- Personal visits to the bank
- Computers

Determine how your bank handles wire transfers and craft your internal controls based on those dynamics. Governments should do the following to mitigate wire transfer fraud:

1. Require the bank to limit daily wire transfer amounts (e.g., $25,000 per day for each employee).
2. Require *two* persons to consummate all wire transfers to external parties—the most important control in my opinion.
3. If the wire transfer request is by phone or by fax, require the bank to call your government back *before* the wire transfer is consummated; banks will obtain the call-back phone number when the bank account or wire capability is established.
4. The bank should require the use of unique passwords to access wire-transfer software. Consider using a bank that provides a security token (small hand-held devices that generate unique identification numbers; these numbers are keyed into the bank software as a part of the transfer request).
5. Restrict the bank accounts from which a wire transfer can be made. Your government may want to specify just one bank account for external wire transfers.

6. Restrict certain bank accounts so that wire transfers can be made only to other bank accounts of the government (e.g., transfer from operating bank account to payroll bank account).
7. Have someone peruse the daily bank account activity using online access. At a minimum, reconcile bank statements in a timely fashion. Large governments should consider reconciling bank accounts more frequently than once a month; some reconcile daily.
8. Require sufficient documentation for all wire transfer journal entries, and require a second-person approval of these journal entries.
9. Consider using a dedicated computer for all wire transfers; do not use this computer for any other purpose. Malware is often picked up by computers as users browse the Internet or click links in emails.
10. Use all bank-provided wire transfer controls for software and hardware.
11. Any transactions over a certain high dollar amount (e.g., $50,000) should have the approval of a high-level governmental administrative officer.
12. Use appropriate firewall and antivirus protection, and update all software patches.

Choosing not to use controls offered by banks may make your government liable if funds are stolen. One commercial company sued its bank when hackers took $440,000 from its bank account with a wire transfer. The judge ruled against the company because it had opted out of control procedures offered by the bank.

If one person can make external wire transfers and journal entries to record those transactions, you have the makings of fraud—soon you may see that employee on Facebook, riding down the old Danube.

PAYROLL FRAUD

While disbursement and purchasing fraud is more prevalent in local governments, theft in the payroll area, when it occurs, can be equally damaging. Lace up your boots, it's time to take our next step down the local government fraud trail: payroll.

In many governments, a limited number of persons (often one or two) handle the entire payroll function. In such situations, appropriate segregation of duties may not exist and fraud can occur.

Common payroll fraud schemes include:
- Duplicate payments
- Ghost employees
- Inflating pay rates and hours worked
- Backdoor thefts of payroll withholdings

After reviewing these schemes, we'll see how you can segregate your payroll duties. But before we delve into the details of payroll fraud, please allow me to state the obvious: Payroll fraud occurs where it's possible, namely in the human resources or payroll department. Again, you're thinking, "Duh?" But I find that auditors all too often don't keep this truth in mind. When you examine W-2s at year-end, first look at those of your payroll staff. When you review your computerized master pay rate file, scrutinize annual wages and hourly rates of payroll personnel. When you consider whether fictitious employees exist, inspect the payroll records of human resource employees.

While payroll fraud is commonly committed by human resources or payroll accountants, it does, at times, occur without the involvement of payroll personnel, such as when departments overstate hours worked.

Duplicate Payments

One common payroll scheme is the issuance of duplicate payroll checks, especially to the payroll clerk or finance director, since they often control payroll disbursements. This is even more prevalent when these persons can also sign payroll checks, whether physically or electronically, or if they make direct deposit payments. Be wary of situations where one person can issue payroll checks (including direct deposits) *and* record the transaction in the general ledger without review by a second party.

Ghost Employees

Almost any discourse about payroll fraud includes a discussion regarding ghost employees (fictitious employees on the payroll), so I won't disappoint.

In order to have a ghost employee, someone must create the employee record or leave a terminated employee in the payroll system. The latter is the more common practice since it's easier to do—no drug test required, for example. By leaving a terminated employee in the payroll system, the fraudster (usually the payroll clerk or finance director) can simply change the terminated employee's bank account number to his own, and with direct deposit, the ghost employee payments are sent to the fraudster's bank account. So how do we prevent and detect the existence of ghost employees?

- Periodically compare each employee in the payroll system to individual personnel files—ghosts don't normally have personnel files.
- Examine any returned W-2s. If the ghost has a ghost address, the W-2 will be returned to the government. Compare returned W-2s to personnel files.
- Don't allow just one person to perform both of the following:
  - the duty of adding or deleting an employee.
  - payroll processing function.

- If possible, have the computerized payroll system generate an email to someone outside the payroll department (e.g., finance director) for each change of address or each person added or deleted from the system. Alternatively, have the system generate a monthly report of all changes to payroll—again going to a reviewer outside of payroll.
- Use a payroll system that requires second-party approval of any key changes to payroll records.

Inflating Pay Rates and Hours Worked

One of the easiest ways to commit payroll theft is to inflate pay rates in the master payroll file. To mitigate this risk, the government should limit who has access to the master pay rate file. Make sure appropriate passwords are established and that those passwords are known only by authorized persons. In addition, all pay rates should be documented in each employee's personnel file. The person authorizing the pay rate should sign and date the approval sheet.

Many small governments use time clocks which are activated by the swipe of an employee's identification card. This is fine, but consider using biometric systems which are more effective in eliminating buddy-punching. Biometric systems read physical features of the employee (e.g., fingerprint). The problem with payroll identification cards is they can be left near the time clock and workmates can clock in for a buddy while that friend is still in bed, enjoying a morning snooze. Another simple preventive measure is to install video cameras at clock-in sites; then if buddy-punching occurs, it will be captured. And the presence of the camera will lessen the temptation.

In local governments, excessive overtime is a common problem. Overtime should be budgeted by department, and the department head should explain the cause of significant variances to the governing body or administrative manager. If overtime exceeds a full-time-equivalent (FTE), it may be prudent to hire an additional employee. But consider that the excess may be a fraud red flag. If overtime exceeds an FTE by multiples (e.g., overtime equals four FTEs), then you have an even greater indication that fraud is occurring—and potentially with the complicity of a department head.

Regardless of the payroll system, supervisors should review and approve the time records for their department—prior to the remittance of these records to accounting. Once the time records are received in accounting, the payroll clerk should review the submitted information for significant variances, *prior* to processing payroll.

Backdoor Thefts of Payroll Withholdings

Another threat is possible: A payroll clerk can intentionally overpay payroll withholding (for the government as a whole), alter his or her W-2 withholdings to include the excess payment, and later receive a tax refund that includes the overpayment. For example, if Gertrude, the payroll clerk, intentionally overpays state tax withholdings by $5,000, she can amend her W-2 so that it reflects the overpayment amount as withheld from her paycheck (though it was not). Once she files her state tax return, she gets an extra $5,000. In effect, she is using the state government as a funnel for her theft. Since payroll tax deposit payments are seldom monitored by a second person, it's an easy way to steal. The potential for this scheme increases if one person processes payroll, files all related payroll tax reporting information, makes payroll withholding payments, and records payroll entries in the general ledger—not uncommon in smaller governments. As a preventive measure, have someone outside of payroll review all W-2s before they are issued, and then have this person mail the W-2s so the payroll clerk cannot make changes after the review.

Segregation of Payroll Duties

Most of these threats can be eliminated or greatly diminished by implementing appropriate segregation of duties. Where possible, the government should segregate the following payroll responsibilities:

- Setting up new employees and deleting terminated employees
- Authorizing wage rates
- Entering or changing pay rates in the accounting system
- Entering time into the accounting system
- Processing and printing of checks (or making direct deposit payments)
- Reconciliation of the payroll bank account

If one person can enter pay rates and time worked, process checks, and reconcile the payroll bank account, the government has the perfect setting for payroll theft. If this person can also set up new employees or remove terminated employees, your risk goes up even more. In such situations, have a second person review and sign off on payroll, or have a periodic audit of your payroll performed.

Be aware that most external auditors do not perform detailed payroll procedures. They normally perform analytical procedures such as comparing budget to actual numbers by department, or they might reconcile 941s to total payroll in the general ledger. Consequently, many payroll frauds may remain undetected, even though an annual audit is performed.

———

CAPITAL ASSET FRAUD

We come to the last transaction cycle we are to examine: capital assets. Airplanes, trucks, ambulances, police cars, trains, bulldozers, and fire trucks sometimes disappear. You're thinking, "How can assets of this physical size simply vanish?" I know it seems impossible. But it happens. Let's see how.

Planes, Trains, and Automobiles

Okay, honestly I've never seen any stories about trains disappearing (I just like the title), but I have seen where jet parts and automobiles vanish. For example, an April 10, 2008 *USA Today* article began with, "Stolen and sensitive U.S. military equipment, including fighter jet parts wanted by Iran... has been available to the highest bidder on popular Internet sales sites." The article went on to say that the equipment, "purchased with taxpayer money," was available for purchase on eBay and Craigslist and included "components from F-14 fighter jets" and a "used Nuclear Biological Chemical protective suit."

While most local governments don't have high-profile thefts like F-14 fighter jet parts, they are, nonetheless, subject to theft of equipment. So how does the theft of capital assets occur?

The main culprit is usually a lack of accountability. Many local governments do not perform periodic inventories of capital assets. Often, equipment is purchased and added to the depreciation schedule, but no one—at a later date—compares this master list of capital assets purchased to what is physically present.

I find that most external auditors (those who render opinions on financial statements) audit the additions and deletions to capital assets but seldom, if ever, audit *existing* capital assets. Consequently, theft of capital assets may go undetected in annual external audits.

Nip It in the Bud

To use the words of the inimitable Barney Fife (my hero), "Nip it in the bud." But how? It's really quite simple, though it can be time consuming.

Just perform an annual inventory of the assets, comparing the master list of capital assets purchased with what is physically present. This annual reconciliation should be performed by someone outside of the department being inventoried. You should also, by policy, assign responsibility for each capital asset to a particular employee. For example, a city should assign responsibility for all public works equipment to the public works director. If any of the equipment in that department is not present, then the director is accountable for the deficiency.

Be aware that some governments receive property without an outlay of cash, such as the receipt of excess federal property and donations received from citizens or nonprofits. Governments also confiscate property (e.g., cars) in crime-related seizures by policing authorities (e.g., a drug raid)—again without an outlay of cash. All property, whether purchased or received at no cost, should be included on the capital asset inventory. Property not accounted for is ripe for theft.

When property is moved from one department to another department, a transfer sheet (signed by the transferring party and the receiving party) should be completed as documentation for the movement of the property and the capital asset records should be updated.

If an annual inventory has not been performed in the past, the government should announce openly that a capital asset inventory policy has been instituted and will be enforced. Accountability is critical. If accountability is not assigned to specific personnel, you will make little progress in mitigating the theft of capital assets.

Capitalization Thresholds

Most governments adopt a capitalization threshold to define the level of purchases that will be added to the depreciation schedule (or capital asset detail). For example, a city might use a $2,000 threshold; capital assets purchased for less than this amount are not capitalized for depreciation purposes—they are expensed when paid. Consequently, these less expensive purchases are often not recorded on the capital asset inventory.

A *greater* danger of theft exists for assets not inventoried. If your government adopts a *depreciation* capitalization threshold (e.g., $2,000), consider maintaining a list of all purchases above a certain *accountability* level (say $250) and assign the responsibility for these lower value items to designated personnel. Continuing with the public works example above, the director would be responsible for all capital assets in his department greater than $250. Maintaining an inventory of these less expensive assets decreases the threat of theft.

Some small dollar capital assets should always be inventoried. Recently, *The Wall Street Journal* reported that the U.S. Marshals Service had lost a few thousand encrypted communication devices. Such devices, in the wrong hands, can allow persons to listen in on policing operations and, as a result, potentially compromise the safety of officers and citizens. And what was the cause of the loss of these devices that ranged in price between $2,000 to $5,000? A lack of appropriate inventorying software and accounting.

Construction Fraud

It's time to build a new governmental building—a courthouse, a public safety complex, a jail. Regardless of the project, the cost can be several million dollars and the complexity, daunting. Governmental leaders know what they desire (a new building) but may not know how to reach the goal safely.

Two factors make construction projects ripe for fraud:

- Big dollars (creates an incentive to steal)
- Complexity of construction (makes it easier to hide fraud)

Three of the primary means of construction fraud are as follows:

- Kickbacks from the contractor to the awarding officials
- Over-billing
- Deficient materials and cutting corners

Kickbacks

Construction kickbacks can come in gifts, trips, cash, and even a house. Yes, a house. A few years ago, I was told about a large construction project (the building of a new county hospital) in which the CEO received a new vacation home—free of charge. The vacation home costs were charged to the hospital construction project. Since the hospital construction project was in excess of $50 million, it was easy to hide the cost of the vacation home.

Once while I was interviewing the CEO at a public hospital, I asked why they had not bid out a major construction project and his response was, "We've always used this construction company and have been satisfied with their work." I could smell the kickback. When relationships between government officials and contractors are cozy, beware.

Over-Billing

Over-billing can occur as a construction company charges more than what is contractually allowable, for expenses unrelated to your project, for improper overhead allocations, for expenses that never occurred, and by not crediting your government for unused materials—just to name a few.

In 2012, one New York construction company was charged with over-billing to "pay foremen one or two hours extra each day for work that was never done" and for "sick days, holidays, and vacation time in violation of its labor agreements." The U.S. Attorney handling the case stated the company had over-billed on "every project over years," resulting in fraud of $19 million.

Deficient Materials and Cutting Corners

Often, construction project costs are fixed by the bidding process, but an *indirect* form of theft may occur in the form of deficient materials, a lack of appropriate bonding, and non-compliance with laws and regulations. The contractor cuts corners to inflate his profit. And given the complexity of most construction projects, these short-cuts can be difficult for the untrained eye to detect. The substandard work, resulting from deficient materials or cutting corners, may not be evident for years, but when the cracks appear in the ceiling, it's too late to deal with the problem.

Mitigating Construction Fraud

The normal process for large construction projects is to secure funding, bid the project, construct the building, and cut the ribbon. Given that fraud can occur in any of these phases (except cutting the ribbon), what can a government do to prevent or mitigate construction fraud?

Hire a construction monitor to represent the government's interest. But isn't the government already paying the contractor to manage the construction project? Yes, but whose interest is most important to the contractor? Isn't there a professional engineer involved? Yes. But, in many cases, this is not enough. When several million dollars are going into a project, it becomes more probable that fraud will occur.

Your hired construction monitor should be given open access to records and to the worksite itself. Working on your behalf, this construction professional will ensure that all phases of the project are performed in the government's best interest, not the contractor's. But doesn't this just add to the cost of the project? Not necessarily. The diminution of waste and fraud can easily offset the cost of a monitoring agent—especially for high-cost projects.

The monitoring agent should be hired at the very beginning of the project, even before design and bidding. To find such a person, check with the National Association for Construction Auditors for potential candidates; see *http://www.thenaca. org/.* Pick two or three, and call references to see how they performed on previous projects.

A monitoring agent is not a silver bullet, but I think hiring such a person will lessen fraud. If you want to minimize the cost of the construction monitor, restrict his work to the highest risk areas (e.g., contract vetting).

Even if you don't use a monitoring agent, at least use a sealed-bid process and open the bids in a public meeting. Thereafter, pay close attention to the change order process.

CHAPTER 4

Detecting Fraud

Your best bet is to prevent fraud, but even your best efforts may fail. Fraud may still occur. And if it does, how do you find it? Pinpointing fraud can be like looking for the proverbial needle in a haystack. Many people, including professional auditors, don't realize that fraud schemes are so numerous. There aren't twenty ways to steal, or fifty, or a hundred. There are, I believe, thousands (although I haven't counted them). My point is, the multitude of schemes makes it difficult to unearth fraud. And remember the average life of a fraud is eighteen months. So as each day passes, dollars are lost. The greater the time, the greater the damages.

As we discussed previously, fraud is often detected by tips or by accident. Many of these "accidents" occur while employees are on vacation. Interestingly, fraud surfaces when a substitute employee performs the vacationing employee's tasks and things just don't add up. Questions are asked. Prior reports are examined. And *bam!* fraud is discovered. So one easy way to detect fraud is to require all accounting personnel to take vacations and to have someone perform the absent employee's duties.

You can, if you have the dollars to do so, hire an outside fraud specialist. But if not, you can perform your own fraud tests (although I recommend hiring a specialist from time to time). While this book is not designed to provide dozens of fraud tests, below I offer a few simple examples that most anyone can perform. Some of these techniques can be performed without a computer while the others require a computer and an electronic spreadsheet (such as Excel).

Receipt Fraud Tests

Here are three receipt fraud tests.

1. Test Adjustments Made to Receivables

Why test?

Theft of cash is commonly achieved by persons writing off (or writing down) receivables and taking cash equal to the adjustment. Receivables (e.g., utility bills) are adjusted to ensure that the customer will not receive a bill that reflects an unpaid balance.

How to test?

Obtain a download of receivable adjustments (decreases of receivable accounts) for a period of time (e.g., two weeks) and see if they were properly authorized. Review the activity with someone outside of the receivables area (e.g., finance director) who is familiar with procedures but who has no access to cash collections.

If there are multiple people with the ability to adjust receivable accounts (quite common in public hospitals), compare weekly or monthly adjustments for each receipting clerk.

Agree receipts created with the bank deposits.

2. Confirm Checks Received

Why test?

When (1) payments are received and the amount was not previously recorded as a receivable, and (2) the payment was not received at a central cash collection area (e.g., rebate checks sent to purchasing agent), an increased risk exists that the checks will be stolen.

How to test?

Determine who provides rebate checks (or other checks commonly received that are not recorded as receivables). Send a confirmation of payments to the paying party and compare the confirmed amounts with activity in the general ledger.

This type of theft is more prone to occur in larger governments where checks are sometimes received by executives (e.g., hospital authorities). The executive receives the check in the mail and keeps it for a while to see if anyone will notice. If anyone inquires about the check, he says, "Oh yeah, I forgot to give it to you. Here it is in my desk." If no one ever inquires about the check, he steals and converts the check to cash.

3. Search for Off-the-Book Theft of Receipts

Why test?

The fraudster may bill for services, taxes, or fines through the government's accounting system, or an alternative set of accounting records, and personally collect the payments.

How to test?

Compare current year revenues with prior years and investigate significant variances. Alternatively, start with original source documents and walk a sample of transactions through revenue recognition, billing, and collection.

Here are two examples of actual off-the-book receipt thefts:

An auditor detected a decrease in police fine revenue in a small city while performing audit planning analytics. Upon digging deeper, he discovered the police chief had two receipt books, one for checks that were appropriately deposited, and a second for cash going into his pocket.

A hospital CFO, while performing reorganization procedures, set up a new bank account specifically for deposit of electronic Medicaid remittances. He established himself as the sole authorized bank account check signer. Strangely, the bank account was never set up in the general ledger. As the Medicaid money was electronically deposited, the CFO used the funds to build a nice home, purchase new cars, and pay for gambling trips.

Disbursement Fraud Tests

Here are six disbursement fraud tests.

1. Test for Duplicate Payments

Why test?

Theft may occur as the accounts payable clerk generates the same check twice, stealing and converting the second check to cash. The second check may be created in a separate check batch—a week or two later. This threat increases if (1) checks are signed electronically or (2) the check signer commonly does not examine supporting documentation and the check payee name.

How to test?

Obtain a download of the full check register in Excel. Sort by dollar amount and vendor name. Investigate same-dollar payments with same-vendor names above a certain threshold (e.g., $25,000).

If you have access to ACL, IDEA, or ActiveData software, you can perform a "same, same, same" test. You want to sort for the same dollar amount, the same invoice number, and the same vendor number. (I recommend ActiveData, an Excel add-in, as a cheaper alternative to ACL and IDEA. Not only is it more economical, it's easier to use. ACL and IDEA are more powerful, but are more costly and have a steeper learning curve.)

If you see duplicate payments, determine where the checks were deposited. If the duplicate check was deposited to an employee's bank account, you probably have fraud. If the duplicate check was deposited to the vendor's bank account, the accounts payable clerk may have accidentally paid the same invoice twice.

2. Review the Accounts Payable Vendor File

Why test?

Fictitious vendor names may mimic real vendor names (e.g., ABC Company is the real vendor name while the fictitious name is ABC Co.). Additionally, the home address of the accounts payable clerk is assigned to the fake vendor (alternatively, P.O. boxes may be used).

The check signer will not recognize the payee name as fictitious.

How to test?

Obtain a download of all vendor names in Excel. Sort by name and visually compare any vendors with similar names. Investigate any near-matches.

If you have access to ACL, IDEA, or ActiveData software, you can perform a "same, same, different" test. You will search the check register for incidences of the same dollar amount, the same invoice number, and a different vendor number. You are looking for duplicate checks. You should not find the same invoice number being paid twice. Many accounting packages will not allow the payment of the same invoice twice, but some accounting packages allow the operator to override the control. If you do find an invoice being paid twice, dig deeper.

3. Check for Fictitious Vendors

Why test?

The accounts payable clerk may add a fictitious vendor (one in which no similar vendor name exists, as was illustrated in the preceding example). The fictitious vendor address? You guessed it: the clerk's home address (or P.O. box).

Pay particular attention to new vendors that provide services (e.g., consulting) rather than physical products (e.g., inventory). Physical products leave audit trails; services, less so.

How to test?

Obtain a download in Excel of new vendors and their addresses for a period of time (e.g., a month or quarter). Google the businesses to check for existence; if necessary, call the vendor. Or ask someone familiar with vendors to review the new-vendor list (preferably someone without vendor setup capabilities).

4. Compare Vendor and Payroll Addresses

Why test?

Those with vendor-setup ability can create fictitious vendors associated with their own home address. If you compare all addresses in the *vendor* file with addresses in the *payroll* file, you may find a match. (Be careful—sometimes the match is legitimate, such as travel checks being processed through accounts payable.) Investigate any suspicious matches.

How to test?

Obtain a download in Excel of (1) vendor names and addresses and (2) payroll names and addresses. Merge the two files; sort the addresses and visually inspect for matches.

5. Scan All Checks for Proper Signatures and Payees

Why test?

Fraudsters will forge signatures or complete checks with improper payees, such as themselves.

How to test?

Pick a period of time (e.g., two months), obtain the related bank statements, and scan the cleared checks for appropriate signatures and payees. Also consider scanning endorsements.

6. Review Checks Falling Just Below Approval Limits

Why test?

Fraudsters will requisition check payments just below purchasing policy thresholds to avoid additional scrutiny. For example, the government might require two signatures on checks above $10,000; the fraudster might requisition a payment to a fictitious vendor for $9,900.

How to test?

Download the check register into Excel and sort checks by payment amount. Review checks made out for amounts just below the purchasing policy threshold, particularly if you see several checks made out to the same vendor and if the authorization for payment comes from the same person (e.g., department head).

CHAPTER 5

Procuring Fraud-Related Audit Services

If you bought this book because you suspect fraud and need to immediately hire a local government auditor, this chapter is for you. But even if you are not in dire straits, you'll find this chapter helpful in securing the services of an outside fraud professional.

In this chapter we'll address the following:

- What an Audit Is (and What It Is Not)
- Solicitation of Fraud-Related Audit Services
- Types of Audits
- Who Performs Governmental Audits

Many times when fraud occurs or is suspected, governments are scrambling to find the fire-alarm "Pull Here" lever. But smoke has filled the room and panic may have set in. Hopefully this is not your situation today, but if it is, let me lend you a hand.

First, you may need to place suspected personnel on administrative leave and contact your attorney. Second, let's look at how your government can obtain audit assistance.

What an Audit Is (and What It Is Not)

Confusion reigns with regard to what an audit is and the type that is needed. For example, I am commonly asked, "Do we need a forensic audit?" Many people do not know that different types of audits exist. And adding to the confusion— each state has its own local government audit rules.

Solicitation of Fraud-Related Audit Services

When fraud is suspected, two gnawing questions arise:

1. Is fraud really occurring?
2. If yes, what's the damage?

And possibly a third: Am I going to be fired?

It's at this point that the government knows it needs professional fraud-related audit services. Next, two more questions arise:

1. Who should I hire?
2. How much will it cost?

The government can pick up the phone and call those who know about fraud audits or they can issue request for proposals (RFPs). They usually do the latter, although I'm not so sure it's the best option. If you can find a reputable, fairminded audit company, hire them. (Ask for at least two references and, of course, rates.) If not, here's some information about issuing fraud-related RFPs.

First let me say that governments may need outside assistance in *preparing* an RFP for fraud-related services. It's not every day that fraud is encountered; consequently, when fraud occurs, governments often struggle with writing the RFP. (Copying your regular audit RFP usually will not work— annual audits and forensic investigators are completely different types of services.)

Another important factor: The government may not want to request an aggregate price for the entire project. Using a low bid is not a good idea for fraud projects. Why? Because in the beginning of the fraud investigation, no one knows how large the project will be.

Most fraud projects should be broken down into two phases:

1. Predication
2. Audit

What is predication? It is the first part of the investigation where the auditor determines whether evidence exists to merit the second phase of the investigation: audit. In the predication phase, the auditor is simply sniffing around to see if more work should be performed.

Once the auditor has completed the predication phase, the government can decide, based on the evidence found, whether or not to proceed.

For the predication phase, the government should consider asking for a maximum price (or range of pricing). The government may desire to request a schedule of hourly rates; those same rates can be used in the second phase of the investigation.

The government should normally use the same firm to perform the two phases of the investigation. So basically whichever firm wins the predication bid would be the auditor for the full project. If the government elects to proceed with the second phase of the project, the audit firm's invoices should reflect the hours worked by staff level, a description of work performed, and the hourly rates. (These details provide transparency in the billing process.)

Types of Audit Services

Let's look at three fraud-related services that governments may request:

1. GAAS audit - opinion on the government's financial statements
2. Forensic audit - preparation for legal proceedings
3. Internal control review - review of accounting procedures and controls

GAAS Audits

Most local government audits are performed by CPA firms in accordance with generally accepted auditing standards (GAAS). The goal of such audits is for the CPA firm to render an opinion on the fairness of the government's presentation of numbers and disclosures. In rendering that opinion, the auditor uses a concept called *materiality*, an idea that is commonly not understood by elected officials and governmental management. The CPA's audit opinion states:

> *In our opinion, the financial statements present fairly, in all material respects...in accordance with accounting principles generally accepted in the United States of America.*

The CPA's audit opinion is saying that the government's numbers are fairly presented above a certain threshold (materiality). For example, an auditor may compute a materiality threshold of $100,000 for a city general fund. This means the auditor may allow for errors or theft in amounts below $100,000 and still issue a clean opinion. The CPA's objective is to perform the audit with this allowance in mind and then render the opinion.

According to ACFE studies, the median-sized governmental fraud is between $80,000 to $100,000. However, GAAS audits may not be designed to search for typical-sized frauds. Many people do not understand this—until it's too late.

Your local government may have been audited for decades, but undetected fraud may have existed for many of those years. Let me say this very plainly: GAAS audits are not designed to detect *all* fraud. So what should a government do if fraud is suspected and a more detailed examination is needed? Depending on the evidence, a forensic audit or an internal control review may be in order.

Forensic Audits

Black's Law Dictionary defines *forensic* as "used in or suitable to courts of law or public debate." Forensic auditing, therefore, is actually litigation support involving preparation for trial. If a government is requesting forensic services, they are asking for assistance in preparing for court proceedings; the request for forensic services also, in an indirect way, means the government has *already* identified fraud—otherwise, the government would not be preparing for trial.

My experience is that many governments request forensic services, not really understanding the term. The government is actually thinking, "We suspect that someone has stolen money, and we need an expert to determine if this is true." May I suggest that governments avoid using the word *forensic* until preparing for trial (after the fraud is discovered). Prematurely using the word *forensic* may saddle the government with a libel or slander suit or, at a minimum, inflame those who are the target of the government's suspicions. A more suitable means of wading into the water is available— an internal control review.

Internal Control Review

Start your fraud investigation as a targeted internal control project. Use terms such as *a review of internal controls* or *a review for cash receipting procedures* (for example). These terms are a Mr. Rogers' kinder, gentler description than *forensic* audit.

The government can obtain fraud-related services (with fewer potential litigation risks) by using wording such as:

The City of Caspian is requesting bids on the review of its cash receipting procedures.

The preceding language is more benign and less accusatory than:

The City of Caspian is requesting forensic auditing services with regard to the City's cash receipting procedures.

This is especially true if only one or two people work in the cash receipting area. Internal control reviews (especially those related to potential fraud) typically are not performed in accordance with GAAS; in other words, no opinion is rendered. (CPAs *can* render opinions on internal controls, but such opinions are seldom issued in relation to governments.) CPAs can perform internal control reviews under the Consulting Standards of the American Institute of Certified Public Accountants (AICPA). Such services are most often provided when the final report is not intended for use by third parties such as a bank. The AICPA Consulting Standards allow the CPA to create a mixture of narratives and exhibits—as a report—that describes and demonstrates the operations of the accounting system and personnel.

Certified Fraud Examiners perform their work under the rules established by the Association of Certified Fraud Examiners (ACFE). Their final reports will also usually be a mixture of narratives and exhibits. Now we will look at who performs local government audits.

Who Performs Local Government Audits

If a local government doesn't understand who audits what, it may unknowingly allow significant governmental operations to go unaudited.

Think of local government audits in terms of a continuum based on the size of operations and funds handled. That continuum, running from smaller to larger governments, is as follows:

1. Self-audit (often by the elected officials)
2. Non-GAAS audits (usually performed by external CPA firms, state audit departments, or the government's internal audit department)
3. GAAS audits (performed by external CPA firms)

Why would some local government operations not be audited?

1. Some state laws exempt smaller governments from audit requirements.
2. Local government officials may believe all operations are audited when they are not.

Many states exempt smaller governments (e.g., cities with less than $200,000 in revenues) from external audit requirements. Sometimes internal audit procedures (e.g., self-audit by elected officials) are performed for these smaller governments—normally, this is not a sound process since elected officials are usually not trained to perform such procedures. These smaller governments should consider hiring an outside audit person or firm to assist, at some level, in the review of the records.

Understand that larger local government audits are most often performed by CPA firms on a contract basis (i.e., the government pays for the audit) or by a state department of audits. Each state provides different audit services based on state laws. In some states, a local government may be audited both by a CPA firm and by state audit officials. More commonly, however, a CPA firm audits the governmental entity and no state level audit is performed, but again, this varies from state to state. For example, in Georgia, most public schools are audited by the Georgia Department of Audits, while counties and cities are audited by CPA firms. In New

York state, the state comptroller's office audits internal controls of local governments—a service not provided by every state.

GAAS audits, whether performed by CPA firms or state agencies, do not always cover every part of a government. For example, an audit of a county government may not include detailed audit procedures directed at agency funds such as a tax office or a probate court. Since an audit opinion may not be rendered with regard to agency funds, local governments may mistakenly believe that all entities, including agency funds, are fully audited, when they are not.

CHAPTER 6

Auditing and Certified Public Accountants

This chapter is for Certified Public Accountants and those who audit governments. If you are not an auditor, feel free to skip this section.

I've heard auditors express strong opinions about their preference for the balance sheet audit approach. My thoughts, offered below, are contrary to those of some of my friends. Next we'll see how fraud can sting auditors, and, lastly, I provide some guidance on understanding and communicating internal control weaknesses.

The Balance Sheet Approach

"Sacred cows make great steaks."[5]

Years after the issuance of the risk-based audit standards, we still see an avoidance of risk assessment procedures. In its place, an old audit friend remains: the pure balance sheet approach.

What is the balance sheet approach? It's the examination of period-end balance sheet totals (the results of accounting processes) rather than the accounting processes themselves.

---

5 Richard Nicolosi.

For example, the auditor might confirm receivables rather than perform a walk-through of billing and collections.

Nailing down (or "beating up") the balance sheet does provide noteworthy audit evidence, but weaknesses do exist in this approach. So what are those weaknesses?

First, the balance sheet approach does not address the income statement; consequently, income statement line items may be misclassified. If the balance sheet is correct, net income—the result of revenues and expenses—must be correct. But revenues and expenses may be misclassified. (I once saw grant revenue of $300,000 netted with related grant expenses, resulting in a $0 impact to revenues and expenses.)

Second, and more importantly, a balance sheet audit does not address some forms of fraudulent reporting of revenues and expenses and some forms of theft. Sure, we can confirm cash and reconcile the balance to the general ledger. So what? If someone steals $1 million in cash receipts, the balance sheet approach will not address the control weaknesses which allowed the theft to occur.

The same is true if a finance director steals money by cutting checks to himself or herself. The accounts payable balance can be reconciled to a detail, and a search for unrecorded liabilities can be performed—typical balance sheet audit steps—but these procedures will not detect theft.

Finally, audit standards require walk-throughs, fraud inquiries, planning analytics, and an understanding of the government. Until these steps are performed, we cannot truly understand the risks that often lie hidden in accounting processes.

I still believe that auditors can save time using a risk-based audit approach. We can gain an understanding of the government and develop an audit plan that addresses risk rather than blindly "beating up the balance sheet." The time-savings occur in the performance of more focused procedures. Also we will mitigate audit risk because we better understand the accounting system. Less time, less risk. Sounds good to me, but slaying the sacred cow (the balance sheet approach) is necessary. I like my steaks medium well. How about you?

When existing fraud is not detected by auditors, the result can be embarrassing and costly—our next topic of discussion.

Fraud Stings Auditor

Through an inside tip, an audit client discovers an employee fraud, and you, the audit engagement partner, receive the following phone call:

> *"George, we just discovered our finance director has stolen about $70,000 per year for the last three years. Since you guys have been doing our audit, I thought I'd call and discuss what we need to do." The caller does not verbally say it, but he intimates, "Where were* **you** *guys?" and "How are you going to resolve this?"*

Your first thought is the amount stolen is immaterial, and you begin to explain that audits are not designed to detect frauds of this size—the first time your client has heard this. It sounds technical, evasive, and hollow. Your client is thinking, "What did I pay you for?" as you are reading his mind and thinking, "Not for this."

The first mistake was not clearly explaining to your client what an audit is, and, more importantly, what it is not.

The ACFE biennial fraud survey notes that most frauds have a life of about 18 months before they are detected, and less than 10% of frauds are detected by external audits. Even if you as the external auditor are properly performing the engagement, the procedures are designed to detect *material* fraud, something your client needs to know before the audit begins.

Your client files a claim with his insurance company in order to recoup the stolen funds, and, at this point, the insurance company contacts you and asks, "May we have a copy of your internal control letter?" You've known all along that significant deficiencies were present, but you've been afraid to communicate the weaknesses in writing, knowing that doing so might jeopardize your relationship with management (those who hired you).

The second mistake was not communicating all significant weaknesses and material weaknesses in writing.

Now things go from bad to worse. The insurance company sues your firm and subpoenas your work papers as they prepare to take you to court. The insurance company's attorney obtains copies of your fraud work for the last three years, and he notes that the three respective audit files have the same fraud inquiry form. All three annual fraud forms reflect your CPA firm interviewed the same two people and noted, "The company has high ethical standards and no known ways exist to commit fraud." No other fraud work exists in the files. In the deposition, the insurance company's attorney asks you four times, "Did you perform any fraud tests other than inquiring of management?" Now you wish you had.

The third mistake was inquiring of the same personnel year after year and not performing annual fraud tests.

Lessons Learned

You now resolve to do the following on all future audits:
- I will explain to my client that an audit does not address immaterial fraud.
- I will communicate all significant control deficiencies and material weaknesses in writing.
- I will perform at least one new fraud test each year, and those tests will relate to control weaknesses noted in planning walk-throughs and inquiries. Additionally, I will perform fraud inquiries of different personnel each year.

Now that we see how important communicating control weaknesses is, let's see when and how it should be done.

Defining Internal Control Weaknesses

How should you categorize a control weakness? Is it a material weakness, a significant deficiency, or something less? Making this determination can be a struggle. The first step in making the determination is to define the terms.

Definitions of Control Weaknesses

1. *Material weakness*. A deficiency, or a combination of deficiencies, in internal control, such that there is a reasonable possibility that a material misstatement of the entity's financial statements will not be prevented, or detected and corrected, on a timely basis
2. *Significant deficiency*. A deficiency, or a combination of deficiencies, in internal control that is less severe than a material weakness yet important enough to merit attention by those charged with governance
3. *Other deficiencies*. Control deficiencies that are not material weaknesses or significant deficiencies

Our next step is to categorize the control weakness.

How to Categorize a Control Weakness

First, ask two questions:

1. Is there a *reasonable possibility* that a misstatement could occur?
2. Could the misstatement be *material*?

If your answer to both questions is yes, the client has a *material weakness*. (By the way, if you propose a material audit adjustment, it's difficult to argue that no material weakness exists. As you write your control letter, consider examining your proposed audit entries.) If your answer to either of the questions is no, ask the following:

Is the weakness important enough to merit the attention of those charged with governance? In other words, are there elected officials who would see the weakness as important?

If the answer is yes, the weakness is a *significant deficiency*.

If the answer is no, the weakness is an *other deficiency*.

Communicating Control Weaknesses

The following deficiencies must be communicated in writing to management and to those charged with governance:

- Material weaknesses
- Significant deficiencies

Other deficiencies (those that are not material weaknesses or significant deficiencies) can be communicated in writing or orally and need only be communicated to management (and not to those charged with governance). The communication must be documented in the audit file. So if you communicate orally, follow up with a memo to the file addressing the person with whom you spoke, what you discussed, and the date the discussion occurred.

Stand-alone management letters are often used to communicate *other deficiencies*. Since no authoritative guidance for management letters exists, you may word such communications as you wish. Also, you may, if you like, include *other deficiencies* in your written communication of significant deficiencies or material weaknesses.

Supplemental Information

I have found that auditors love checklists. Below you'll find two checklists (one for very small governments and the other for larger governments) and finally, a summary list of helpful fraud resources.

Fraud Prevention for (Very) Small Governments

Most governments don't realize that external audits are *not* designed to detect *immaterial fraud* (*immaterial* can be tens of thousands of dollars—sometimes even more). Such governments may incorrectly believe that a clean opinion means no fraud is occurring—this is a mistake. External financial statement opinion audits are not designed to look for fraud at immaterial levels. *Even if your government has an external audit, consider implementing fraud prevention ideas.*

In a typical small government accounting setting, the city of In Between (as in: *in between two stop lights*) has a mayor and three council members. The city has one bookkeeper (we'll call him Dale) who orders and receives all purchased items; he writes all checks, reconciles bank statements, and keys all transactions into the accounting system. Dale also receipts all collections and makes all deposits. Mayor Chester signs all checks (vendor and payroll). (In a long-standing tradition, the mayor also graces the city Christmas parade float as Santa Claus.) With so little segregation of duties, what can be done?

The smaller the government, the *greater* the need for fraud prevention—even if Santa Claus is involved. And yet, these are the governments that most often don't have the resources—whether money to pay for outside assistance or employees to segregate duties—to prevent fraud. Here are a few ideas for even the smallest of governments.

First, let's look at *lower cost* options:

1. Have all bank statements mailed directly to Mayor Chester who will open and inspect the bank statement activity prior to providing the bank statements to Dale. Alternatively, provide online access to Mayor Chester who reviews bank statement activity and signs a monthly memo documenting his review.

2. Once or twice a year, have council members pick two months at random (e.g., May and September) and review key bank statement activity (e.g., the operating and payroll accounts).

3. Once or twice a year, have council members randomly select checks (e.g., 10 vendor checks and 10 payroll checks) and review supporting documentation (e.g., invoices and time sheets).

4. Once or twice a year, have the mayor and council review receipt collections and related documentation (e.g., for two days of deposits); agree receipts to bank deposits and to the general ledger.

5. Provide monthly budget-to-actual reports to the mayor and council.

6. Provide monthly payroll overtime summaries to the mayor and council.

7. Do not allow Dale to sign checks.

8. Require two signatures on checks above a certain level (e.g., $5,000); have two of the council members (in addition to the mayor) on the bank signature cards; supporting documentation (e.g., invoice) should be provided to check signers for review.

9. Require Mayor Chester *and* Dale to authorize any wire transfers.

10. Have Dale provide the mayor with monthly bank reconciliations; the mayor should document his review (e.g., initial the reconciliation).

11. Don't provide Dale with a credit card.

12. If Dale is provided a credit card, provide him with one card and use a low maximum credit limit (e.g., $1,000). Dale's credit card statements should be provided to the mayor when he signs the related check for payment.

13. Use a centralized receipting location, if possible. Receipts should always be written upon collection of a payment. Restrictively endorse all checks as they are received.

Now let's examine some *higher cost* options (that are usually more effective):

1. Have an outside CPA or Certified Fraud Examiner (CFE) perform the receipting and payment tests listed above.

2. Have an outside CPA or CFE map your internal control system and make system-design recommendations.

3. Have an outside CPA or CFE make surprise unannounced visits (e.g., twice per year) and examine the receipting, payroll, and payment systems. At the beginning of the year, tell Dale that the surprise visits will occur (details of what will be tested should not be communicated to Dale).

4. Install a security camera to record all of Dale's collection and receipting activity.

5. Purchase a fidelity bond to cover elected officials and Dale.

Keep in mind that you can limit the cost of the outside CPA—simply include contract limits for the project. The contract might read *Surprise audit of vendor payments with cost limited to $1,500*. Try to contract with a CPA or CFE with governmental experience. The surprise audits and the fidelity bond recommendations are, in my opinion, the most important considerations.

Some states audit local governments specifically for fraud; consequently, if your local government is frequently audited by a state agency, the need to hire an outside fraud professional is lessened.

Local Governments Internal Control Checklist

Here's a more extensive list of internal controls that I recommend for local governments. The checklist is not intended to be a comprehensive list, but one designed to provide basic fraud-prevention guidance. Every accounting system is different, so use these ideas as they are applicable to your government and modify as necessary.

General Controls

1. Have bank statements mailed directly to someone outside of accounting. The recipient should peruse bank statement activity before providing it to accounting.
2. Perform surprise audits (use an outside CPA or CFE if possible).
3. Elected officials and management should review monthly budget-to-actual reports (and other pertinent financial reports).

4. Map internal control processes by transaction cycle (preferably done by a seasoned CPA). Once complete, provide the map to all employees involved in each cycle. When control weaknesses exist, institute additional controls (see step 11 below).
5. Implement a whistleblower program (preferably using an outside whistleblower company).
6. Reconcile bank statements monthly (have a second person review and initial the reconciliation).
7. Purchase fidelity bond coverage (based on risk exposure).
8. Periodically request from the government's bank a list of all bank accounts in the name of the government or with the government's federal tax I.D. number. Compare the list to bank accounts set up in the general ledger.
9. Secure computer access physically (e.g., locked doors) and electronically (e.g., passwords).
10. Do not allow the electronic transmission (e.g., email) of sensitive data (e.g., social security numbers) without the use of protected transmission technology (e.g., Sharefile). Create an electronic transmission policy and train your staff accordingly.
11. Where possible, segregate who:
    a. Authorizes transactions.
    b. Records transactions.
    c. Reconciles records.
    d. Has custody of assets.

When segregation of duties is not possible, require documented second-person reviews and/or surprise audits.

Cash Receipts and Billing Controls
1. Use a centralized cash collection location (when possible).

2. Assign each cash drawer to a separate person and require daily reconciliation to receipts. Require a second-person review.

3. Deposit cash timely (preferably daily). Require composition of cash and checks to be listed on each deposit ticket to help prevent check-for-cash substitution.

4. Immediately issue a receipt for each payment received. A duplicate of the receipt or electronic record of the receipt is to be retained by the government. Restrictively endorse all checks upon receipt (meaning endorse each check with "For Deposit Only").

5. Supervisor should review receipting personnel adjustments made to accounts receivable.

6. Do not allow the cashing of personal checks from cash drawers.

7. If possible, provide the government's administrative office (e.g., county commissioners' finance department) with electronic viewing rights for all decentralized receipting locations (e.g., landfill).

8. Require the transfer of money from decentralized collection areas on a daily basis. The government's administrative office (e.g., county commissioners' finance department) should provide a receipt to each transferring location (e.g., landfill).

9. Limit the number of bank accounts.

10. Periodically perform surprise audits of receipting areas (including those in outlying areas).

11. The person reconciling the bank statements should not be involved in cash collections.

Disbursements and Purchasing Controls

1. Guard all check stock as though it were cash.

2. Do not allow hand-written checks except in emergencies; only issue checks through the computerized system. If hand-written checks are issued, have a second person create and post the related journal entry.

3. If checks are hand-signed, require documentation (e.g., invoices, purchase orders) be provided to the authorized check signer.
4. Signed vendor checks should not be returned to those who authorized the payment. Instead, mail checks directly to vendors.
5. Do not allow the signing of blank checks. Do not allow the use of signature stamps.
6. Limit check signing authorization to as few people as possible.
7. If checks are signed electronically, limit access to check-signing equipment.
8. Restrict check signer access to accounting records, cash receipts, and bank reconciliations (it is best for check signers not to be a part of the accounting department).
9. Separate bank reconciliation duties from disbursement responsibilities.
10. Restrict access to vendor master file.
11. Require a street address and a Social Security or tax I.D. number for each vendor added to the accounts payable vendor list (P.O. box numbers without a street address should not be accepted).
12. Persons who can add vendors to the vendor master file should not also sign checks. If it's not possible to segregate these duties, perform surprise audits or second-person reviews of disbursements.
13. Compare employee payroll addresses with vendor addresses for potential fictitious vendors (usually performed using electronic audit tools such as IDEA or ACL).
14. Separate purchase order issuance from data-entry duties. Restrict access to purchase order documents.
15. Require two employees to approve each wire transfer.
16. Persons who authorize wire transfers should not make related accounting entries.

17. Require a documented bidding process for larger purchases (and sealed bids for significant purchases or contracts). Specify procedures for evaluating and awarding contracts.

18. Limit the number of credit cards and the amount that can be charged on each card. Allow only one person to use each credit card and require receipts for all purchases.

19. Consider the use of positive-pay (the government periodically sends an electronic list of all checks issued to the bank; checks received by the bank are compared to the list provided by the government; checks not matching the list are not accepted by the bank).

Payroll Controls

1. Provide a departmental overtime budget/expense report to governing body or relevant committee.

2. Use direct deposit for payroll checks.

3. Payroll rates keyed into the payroll system must be supported by proper authorization in the employee personnel file.

4. Immediately remove terminated employees from the payroll system.

5. Use biometric time clocks to eliminate buddy-punching.

6. Time cards should be approved by department heads.

7. Check for duplicate direct-deposit bank account numbers.

8. Overtime should be authorized in writing by department head or designee (before payment is made).

9. Persons who control modifications to the payroll system (e.g., addition of a new employee, changes to pay rates) should not also sign checks. If it's not possible to segregate these duties, perform surprise audits or second-person reviews of payroll transactions.

10. Periodically audit payroll deductions to ensure appropriate parties are paid.
11. Do not pay wages in cash.
12. Review cleared payroll checks for double endorsements (one for forged signature and a second for account name into which check is deposited).
13. Reconcile payroll bank account in a timely manner. The person reconciling the account should not be involved in the disbursement process.
14. Compare payroll expenses with budgeted amounts by department.
15. Consider outsourcing payroll duties as a means to segregating duties.

Capital Asset Controls

1. Maintain an inventory of all capital assets. Include:
   a. Date of purchase.
   b. Full description of the capital asset.
   c. Department to which the asset is assigned.
   d. General ledger account to which the asset is assigned.
2. Tag all property so assets belonging to the government are apparent.
3. Assign responsibility for the capital asset inventory to department heads or their designees.
4. Perform annual inspections of capital assets by reconciling the capital asset inventory to physical assets in each department. Unexplained losses of capital assets should be documented and provided to the governing body.
5. Reconcile the capital asset inventory to general ledger accounts (e.g., vehicles).
6. Develop and use capital asset transfer forms. Have transfer forms signed by department head transferring and the department head receiving the capital asset.

7. Develop a capitalization threshold (e.g., $5,000) to determine the value of purchases to be recorded as capital assets. All assets less than the threshold should be expensed.
8. Maintain a second inventory of items less than the capitalization threshold (e.g., computers, guns in the police department, cell phones, pagers). Perform same reconciliation procedures as specified in step 4.
9. Record all donated or confiscated property received by the government in the capital asset inventory. Record assets received at fair value on the date of donation or confiscation.
10. Require multiple bids for capital assets purchased over certain dollar levels. Have a second party periodically call the bidders to ensure they are legitimate.
11. Create a capital asset disposal policy specifying:
    a. How to document the disposal/sale; create and use a disposal/sale form.
    b. To whom the disposal/sale paperwork should be provided.
    c. Documentation of who received the property along with contact information.
    d. Require the sale of property by open bid for asset values over specified dollar levels. Advertise in the local paper if property is to be sold at local government facility.
    e. Require written approval before capital assets are offered for sale or disposal.
    f. Require written approval from a senior local government official or governing body for any capital asset donated to outside entities. Check with your legal counsel about the legality of donating property.

12. Require police enforcement (e.g., police department) to inventory all confiscated capital assets (e.g., vehicles). Require police enforcement to provide sale or disposal documentation to appropriate governmental officials.
13. Bid all major construction projects. Require sealed bids that are opened in a public meeting.
14. Hire an independent construction expert to monitor the construction project—particularly for large construction projects (e.g., new courthouse or new jail).
15. Create a gratuities policy prohibiting gifts to persons with purchasing authority.
16. Restrict access to capital assets during nonwork hours. Prohibit personal use of capital assets.
17. Restrict access to capital asset property records. Segregate record-keeping duties from purchasing and disposal duties or periodically hire an external auditor to review the capital asset records.

Local Government Fraud Resource List

Here's a list of books, articles, reports, Internet groups, and blogs that will provide you with additional fraud information.

Books:
- *Fraud and Abuse in Nonprofit Organizations: A Guide to Prevention and Detection* by Gerald Zack
- *Forensic Analytics* by Mark J. Nigrini
- *Corporate Fraud Handbook* by Joseph T. Wells

Reports:
- *Report to the Nations on Occupational Fraud and Abuse* by the Association of Certified Fraud Examiners

Internet Groups:
- LinkedIn Governmental and Nonprofit Auditing Group

- LinkedIn Association of Certified Fraud Examiners Group

Fraud-Related Audit Groups:
- Association of Certified Fraud Examiners
- National Association of Construction Auditors
- The Institute of Internal Auditors

Fraud-Related Blogs:
- *CPA-Scribo.com* by Charles Hall
- *Attestationupdate.com* by James Ulvog
- *Theprosandthecons.com* by Gary Zeune

Internet Search:
- *Spokeo.com*—Search for people
- *Ebay.com*—Search for government equipment
- Way Back Machine—Cached (historical) images of websites

Documents:
- Sample Fraud Policy by the Association of Certified Fraud Examiners (ACFE)
- Fraud Prevention Checklist by the ACFE

Fraud Software:
- ActiveData—a moderately-priced and nicely designed Excel add-in
- ACL—high-end fraud software; more challenging to use than ActiveData, but more powerful
- IDEA—high-end fraud software; more challenging to use than ActiveData, but more powerful

Acknowledgment

Ithank those who assisted me in proofing: Donna Pennell, Jean Spinks, and Spencer Hall. I appreciate your patience with me and for your valuable guidance. Obviously, I needed your help. Also, thanks to Michael Koiner for the cover and block production. You made my ragged work look nice. Thank you for your hard work and creativity.

Bibliography

American Institute of Certified Public Accountants. 2012. "Communicating Internal Control Related Matters Identified in an Audit." AU-C Section 265.

Association of Certified Fraud Examiners. *Report to the Nations on Occupational Fraud and Abuse*. Austin, TX: ACFE 2012.

Barrett, Devlin. 2013. "Marshals Lose Track of Encrypted Radios Worth Millions." *The Wall Street Journal*, July 21.

Campbell, James. 2012. "Firm to Pay $56.5 Million in Fraud Case." *The Wall Street Journal*, April 25.

Grimm, Andy, and Jenco, Melissa. 2012. "Small Town Rocked by $30 Million Theft Case." *Chicago Tribune*, April 18.

Jenco, Melissa. 2013. "Dixon to Get $40 Million in Settlement of Embezzlement Case." *Chicago Tribune*, September 25.

Meisner, Jason. 2013. "Prosecutors Seek up to 20-Year Sentence for Ex-Dixon Comptroller Convicted of Stealing Nearly $54 Million." *Chicago Tribune*, February 7.

Roberts, Kate. 2000. "Cancer Exec Turns Self In, Wanted on $6.9 Million Embezzlement Charge." *The Associated Press*, June 10.

Simmons, Christine. 2008. "Stolen Military Equipment Found on eBay." *USA Today*, April 10.

U.S. Census Bureau. 2002. "2002 Census of Governments." July.

Wisniewski, Mary. 2013. "Court Sides with BankCorpSouth Against Wire Transfer Fraud Victim." *American Banker*, April 5.

Author Information

We all know the story of Cinderella and the power of transformation (pumpkins turning into carriages and such). My change, while not as magical, was dramatic nonetheless.

Growing up in the 1960s, I was a south Georgia farm boy, who never dreamed that one day I'd be a forensic accountant. In the early 80s, I found myself majoring in accounting (of all things). In 1985 I performed my first governmental audit. From there, I performed hundreds of such engagements. During those years, I gained an interest—I might even say a *love*—for local government audits (sounds strange, but it's true).

It was during this time that I kept bumping into fraud. I saw the rich, the poor, the educated, the uneducated, the powerful, and the powerless—all steal. At times I felt pity, and, at other times, anger—depending on the reason for the theft. And at other times I felt fear—the thief intimating: *I might hurt you* (and I'm a little guy, so this would not be hard to do). In the midst of the pity, anger, and fear, I gained a passion for preventing fraud.

So my transformation was from a freckle-faced farm boy to gray-haired fraud fighter. In 1987 I became a CPA and in 2004, a Certified Fraud Examiner. I am the quality control partner for McNair, McLemore, Middlebrooks & Co., LLC, where I provide accounting and auditing assistance to our partners and staff. I also provide audit and consulting services to local governments, nonprofit organizations, and small businesses.

I blog about fraud, auditing, and accounting issues at *www.cpa-scribo.com*, and often speak at professional training events—usually about this crazy thing called fraud. If I can be of assistance to you, please email me at *chall@mmmcpa.com*.

72095751R00063

Made in the USA
Columbia, SC
14 June 2017